GLOBALVIEWPOINTS

Workers' Rights

Other Books of Related Interest:

Current Controveries Series
Illegal Immigration

Global Viewpoints Series
Democracy

Discrimination

Human Rights

Human Trafficking

Issues That Concern You Series
Child Labor

Opposing Viewpoints Series
Gays in the Military

Illegal Immigration

The US Latino Community

GLOBALVIEWPOINTS

Workers' Rights

Noah Berlatsky, Book Editor

GREENHAVEN PRESS
A part of Gale, Cengage Learning

GALE
CENGAGE Learning·

Detroit • New York • San Francisco • New Haven, Conn • Waterville, Maine • London

Elizabeth Des Chenes, *Managing Editor*

© 2012 Greenhaven Press, a part of Gale, Cengage Learning

Gale and Greenhaven Press are registered trademarks used herein under license.

For more information, contact:
Greenhaven Press
27500 Drake Rd.
Farmington Hills, MI 48331-3535
Or you can visit our Internet site at gale.cengage.com

For product information and technology assistance, contact us at

Gale Customer Support, 1-800-877-4253
For permission to use material from this text or product, submit all requests online at www.cengage.com/permissions

Further permissions questions can be emailed to permissionrequest@cengage.com

Articles in Greenhaven Press anthologies are often edited for length to meet page requirements. In addition, original titles of these works are changed to clearly present the main thesis and to explicitly indicate the author's opinion. Every effort is made to ensure that Greenhaven Press accurately reflects the original intent of the authors. Every effort has been made to trace the owners of copyrighted material.

Cover image copyright © Charles O'Rear/Corbis.

LIBRARY OF CONGRESS CATALOGING-IN-PUBLICATION DATA

Workers' rights / Noah Berlatsky, book editor.
p. cm. -- (Global viewpoints)
Includes bibliographical references and index.
ISBN 978-0-7377-5668-5 (hardcover) -- ISBN 978-0-7377-5669-2 (pbk.)
1. Employee rights. 2. Human rights. I. Berlatsky, Noah.
HD6971.8.W667 2012
331.01'1--dc23

2011041395

Printed in the United States of America
1 2 3 4 5   16 15 14 13 12

FD084

Contents

Chapter 2: Unions and Collective Bargaining

Chapter 3: Workplace Discrimination

Chapter 4: Migrant and Slave Labor

Japanese internships for foreign workers offered by companies can provide valuable experience. However, a government foreign training program for foreign workers is exploitative and unjust.

Foreword

"The problems of all of humanity can only be solved by all of humanity."
—Swiss author Friedrich Dürrenmatt

Global interdependence has become an undeniable reality. Mass media and technology have increased worldwide access to information and created a society of global citizens. Understanding and navigating this global community is a challenge, requiring a high degree of information literacy and a new level of learning sophistication.

Building on the success of its flagship series, Opposing Viewpoints, Greenhaven Press has created the Global Viewpoints series to examine a broad range of current, often controversial topics of worldwide importance from a variety of international perspectives. Providing students and other readers with the information they need to explore global connections and think critically about worldwide implications, each Global Viewpoints volume offers a panoramic view of a topic of widespread significance.

Drugs, famine, immigration—a broad, international treatment is essential to do justice to social, environmental, health, and political issues such as these. Junior high, high school, and early college students, as well as general readers, can all use Global Viewpoints anthologies to discern the complexities relating to each issue. Readers will be able to examine unique national perspectives while, at the same time, appreciating the interconnectedness that global priorities bring to all nations and cultures.

Material in each volume is selected from a diverse range of sources, including journals, magazines, newspapers, nonfiction books, speeches, government documents, pamphlets, organization newsletters, and position papers. Global Viewpoints is truly global, with material drawn primarily from international sources available in English and secondarily from US sources with extensive international coverage.

Features of each volume in the Global Viewpoints series include:

- An **annotated table of contents** that provides a brief summary of each essay in the volume, including the name of the country or area covered in the essay.

- An **introduction** specific to the volume topic.

- A **world map** to help readers locate the countries or areas covered in the essays.

- For each viewpoint, an **introduction** that contains notes about the author and source of the viewpoint explains why material from the specific country is being presented, summarizes the main points of the viewpoint, and offers three **guided reading questions** to aid in understanding and comprehension.

- **For further discussion** questions that promote critical thinking by asking the reader to compare and contrast aspects of the viewpoints or draw conclusions about perspectives and arguments.

- A worldwide list of **organizations to contact** for readers seeking additional information.

- A **periodical bibliography** for each chapter and a **bibliography of books** on the volume topic to aid in further research.

- A comprehensive **subject index** to offer access to people, places, events, and subjects cited in the text, with the countries covered in the viewpoints highlighted.

Global Viewpoints is designed for a broad spectrum of readers who want to learn more about current events, history, political science, government, international relations, economics, environmental science, world cultures, and sociology—students doing research for class assignments or debates, teachers and faculty seeking to supplement course materials, and others wanting to understand current issues better. By presenting how people in various countries perceive the root causes, current consequences, and proposed solutions to worldwide challenges, Global Viewpoints volumes offer readers opportunities to enhance their global awareness and their knowledge of cultures worldwide.

Introduction

"The persistence of child labour is one of the biggest failures of development efforts."

—*Juan Somavia,*
in preface to Accelerating Action
Against Child Labour: Global Report
Under the Follow-Up to the
ILO Declaration on Fundamental
Principles and Rights at Work,
International Labour Organization, 2010

Some of the most exploited and abused workers are children. UNICEF, the United Nations Children's Fund, in an article on its website, estimates that there are 158 million children between the ages of five and fourteen, or one in six children in the world, involved in child labor. UNICEF notes that many of these jobs involve hazardous conditions. Girls in particular are often employed in domestic labor, and UNICEF notes, "Millions of girls who work as domestic servants are especially vulnerable to exploitation and abuse."

One region that has a serious problem with child labor is Africa. While child labor worldwide is falling, sub-Saharan Africa has not seen a similar decrease. Instead, "more than one in four children below age 14 works," a percentage similar to the world average from 1960, writes Michael Wines in an August 24, 2006, *New York Times* article. Wines adds that children work not only as domestic workers or gardeners, but also as "prostitutes, miners, construction workers, pesticide sprayers, haulers, street vendors, full-time servants, and they are not necessarily even paid for their labor."

Child labor is especially prevalent on West African cocoa farms, where beans are harvested for chocolate. In countries like Côte d'Ivoire, children work long hours in the fields with machetes, exposed to pesticides and hauling heavy loads. Despite government legislation in Côte d'Ivoire, and despite promises from chocolate companies like Nestlé, Hershey's, and Cargill, "today child workers, many under the age of 10, are everywhere," Christian Parenti notes in a February 15, 2008, essay for CNNMoney.com. "Sometimes they're visibly scarred from their work. In the village of Lilo a young boy carrying a machete ambled along a road with a bandaged shin. He said he had cut his leg toiling in a cocoa patch."

Child labor is a problem in other parts of the world as well. For instance, in the Philippines, children, especially girls, are forced into domestic work and prostitution. They are also sometimes recruited to serve as soldiers by terrorist and anti-government organizations. They may also be "involved in compressor mining to extract gold, which requires them to dive into pools of mud using an oxygen tube," explains Jerry E. Esplanada in a January 21, 2011, article at Inquirer.net. Similarly, in an October 12, 2009, article at Global Politician, Bhuwan Thapaliya states that "45.2% of Nepali children are economically active according to the International Labour Organization [ILO]. Child labor is a common phenomenon in Nepal and an ILO report states that 127,000 children are trapped in the 'worst forms of child labor' in Nepal."

Child labor continues to exist in Western countries as well, especially in agriculture. A December 8, 2010, article in the *Socjournal* notes,

> In order to keep food prices at a global competitive level the agricultural industry in the US evolved to using immigrants (mostly from Central and South America) for the manual labor as they are more willing to work for low compensation often being less than the minimum wage. This may not be a surprise to many but what most people don't know is that young children are part of this group too; we're talking about 400,000 children working in agricultural fields.

Why does child labor persist? Michael Wines, in discussing child labor in sub-Saharan Africa, states that some children are trafficked, or kidnapped, and forced to work. However, Wines argues that in most cases, children work not from threat of force, but rather because of poverty and the need to make money for their families. The article in the *Socjournal* also insists that in discussing migrant children working in US fields, "we are not talking about children being forced to work." Rather, the author says, children feel they must work to help their families out of poverty. An article at the Child Labor Public Education Project website titled "Causes of Child Labor" agrees that "poor children and their families may rely upon child labor in order to improve their chances of attaining basic necessities."

The Child Labor Public Education Project also discusses other causes of child labor, however. Among these is a lack of educational opportunities. For instance, Nita J. Kulkarni in a November 15, 2007, blog post at *A Wide Angle View of India* writes that "the truth is that many parents feel that it's useless sending their kids to school as there is no guarantee of a job at the end of it. Not because there is a dearth of jobs but because the quality of education provided in municipal schools (where the majority of poor study) is abysmal." Kulkarni notes that schools lack textbooks and have high student-teacher ratios and poorly paid teachers. She adds that "kids in municipal schools also *face* more corporal punishment and girls *can* be sexually harassed." For all of these reasons, Kulkarni concludes, parents may decide that it makes more sense for their children to begin work than it does for them to stay in school.

The Child Labor Public Education Project also argues that the elimination of child labor is in part dependent on strengthening workers' rights overall. "Workers' abilities to organize unions affect the international protection of core labor standards, including child labor. Attacks on workers' abilities to organize make it more difficult to improve labor standards and living standards in order to eliminate child labor."

Some evidence suggests that globalization may contribute to increases in child labor. Chris Milton, writing at TheEnvironmentSite.org on June 20, 2011, notes that researchers have found that countries open to globalization often experience higher rates of child labor. Milton explains this by arguing that foreign companies build factories in poor areas. "Naturally, when the jobs arrive all the households in the region want to have a piece of the action so the Dads and Mums trek off to try and get a job, and quite often the children get involved too, . . . after all, trebling the household income seems like quite a sweet deal doesn't it?" Professor Susan Ariel Aaronson, writing at Global Politician, agrees that "pressure of globalization has led to child trafficking and forced labor." However, she argues that "similar global pressure from public opinion can also put an end to the practice." She holds out hope that as countries enter into the global network of trade, they will become more open to global sentiment against child labor as well.

The remainder of this book looks at other issues surrounding workers' rights in chapters dealing with labor regulations worldwide, unions and collective bargaining, workplace discrimination, and migrant and slave labor. The authors present different viewpoints on what rights workers should have and how those rights should be balanced with the rights of others and with economic needs.

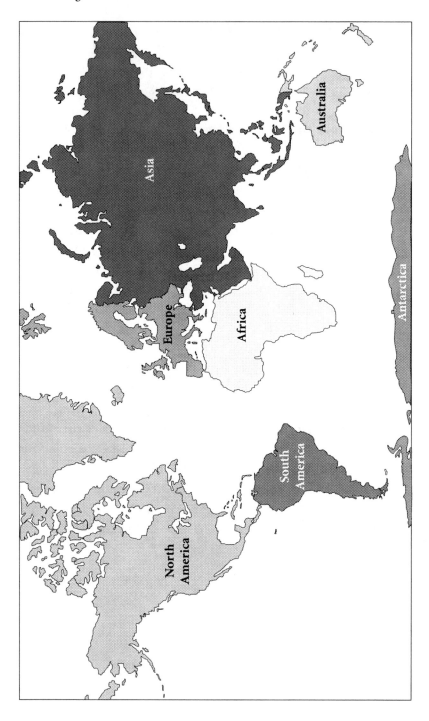

GLOBALVIEWPOINTS

CHAPTER 1

Labor
Regulations Worldwide

In Brazil, Excessive Labor Regulations Harm Employers and Workers

Economist

The Economist *is a British news and business magazine. In the following viewpoint, the* Economist *argues that Brazil's labor laws are outdated and create unnecessary barriers for both employers and workers. The labor laws discourage investment, and their enforcement costs the Brazilian economy billions, says the* Economist. *The laws are so restrictive that some of Brazil's unions are organizing against them; however, the author concludes, the prospect for major reform in the near future seems small.*

As you read, consider the following questions:

1. How many Brazilians opened cases against their employers in labor courts in 2009, according to the *Economist*?

2. What does the *Economist* say derailed reform of labor laws during Luiz Inácio Lula da Silva's presidency?

3. According to the *Economist*, why is the ABC metalworkers' union interested in revising Brazil's labor laws?

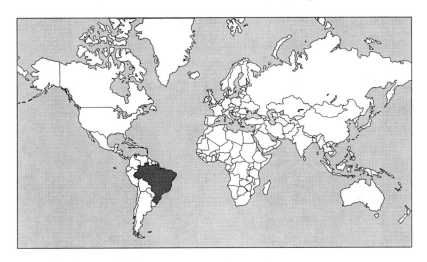

In 1994 Ricardo Lemos (not his real name) and two friends bought a chain of pharmacies in Pernambuco, in Brazil's northeast. Immediately afterwards they were taken to court by four former employees of the pharmacies who claimed they were owed 500,000 reais (then $570,000) for overtime and holidays. Since the new owners lacked the payroll records, the labour court ruled against them—even though they had only just bought the business and the claimants had been in charge of payroll and work scheduling. The court froze their bank accounts, so they had to close the stores, with 35 redundancies [layoffs]. Seventeen years later three of the cases have been settled, for a total of 191,000 reais. The last drags on as the claimant's widow and son squabble over how much to accept.

Costly Labor Laws

Mr Lemos and his partners fell afoul of Brazil's labour laws, a collection of workers' rights set out in 900 articles, some written into the country's constitution. They were originally derived from the corporatist labour code of [fascist dictator Benito] Mussolini's Italy. They are costly: redundancies "without just cause" attract a fine of 4% of the total amount the worker has ever earned, for example. (Neither a lazy employee nor a

21

bankrupt employer constitutes just cause.) Some are oddly specific: for example, annual leave can only be taken in one or two chunks, neither of less than ten days. In 2009, 2.1m [million] Brazilians opened cases against their employers in the labour courts. These courts rarely side with employers. The annual cost of running this branch of the judiciary is over 10 billion reais ($6 billion).

Businessmen have long complained that these onerous labour laws, together with high payroll taxes, put them off hiring and push them to pay under the table when they do. When Luiz Inácio Lula da Silva, a former union leader, became Brazil's president in 2003, they hoped he would be better placed than his predecessors to persuade workers that looser rules would be better for them. But scandals in his first term derailed these and other hoped-for reforms. More recently, as Brazil's economy has boomed, with record numbers of jobs created, the need for change has seemed less pressing. The laws are "very up-to-date", the labour minister, Carlos Lupi, said in December [2010]. He wants firing workers to become still pricier.

Businessmen have long complained that these onerous labour laws ... put them off hiring and push them to pay under the table when they do.

That many of the new jobs are formal (i.e., legally registered) is despite, rather than because of, the labour laws. The trend to formalization is largely a result of the greater availability of bank credit and equity capital on the one hand, and recent changes that make it easier to register microbusinesses on the other. And it coexists with two long-standing Brazilian weaknesses: high job turnover and low productivity growth.

Unusually Burdensome Labor Regulations

Labor regulations in Brazil are the 11th most restrictive in the world. Unusually burdensome legal regulations impede hiring in the formal sector and create problems for firms wishing to adjust their employees' hours of employment.... In addition, firms must pay a quarter of a worker's average salary in hiring costs and pay the equivalent of three years of wages when they fire a worker, three times the regional average. It is not surprising, therefore, that labor regulation is among the top five constraints cited by Brazilian businesses and that some 88 percent of managers would change the size of their labor force if they faced no restrictions on worker dismissals, severance payments, and so forth. The overwhelming proportion of those respondents report that a relaxation of labor rules would cause them to increase the number of workers they employ. Additional evidence indicates that employers are reticent to hire more skilled, and more expensive, workers, since the costs of labor legislation outweigh the benefits of higher labor production. A reduction in costly labor legislation could lead to both an increase in employment and a change in the composition of the labor force toward a higher percentage of skilled workers.

Qimiao Fan, José Guilherme Reis,
Michael Jarvis, Andrew Beath, and Kathrin Frauscher,
The Investment Climate in Brazil, India, and South Africa:
A Comparison of Approaches for Sustaining
Economic Growth in Emerging Economies.
Washington, DC: World Bank Publications, 2008.

Unions for Reform

Gustavo Gonzaga, an economist at Rio de Janeiro's Catholic University, notes that a remarkable one-third of Brazilian workers are made redundant each year, a fact he attributes in part to the labour laws themselves. These are extraordinarily rigid: They prevent bosses and workers from negotiating changes in terms and conditions, even if they are mutually agreeable. They also give workers powerful incentives to be sacked rather than resign. Generous and poorly designed severance payments cause conflict, Mr Gonzaga says, and encourage workers to move frequently. That churn affects productivity, as employers prefer not to spend on training only to see their investment walk away.

Recently, the cause of reform has gained a surprising recruit: the very trade union that Lula himself once led. The ABC metalworkers' union, which represents 100,000 workers in the industrial suburbs of São Paulo, is trying to make union-negotiated agreements binding in the labour courts. At present unions in Brazil cannot strike the sort of deals that are common elsewhere, such as accepting pay cuts during downturns in return for no job losses, since individual workers may later ask the labour courts to unpick them. Hélio Zylberstajn, the president of the Brazilian Institute of Employment and Labour Relations, a study group, thinks the initiative is promising. Unions with the power to negotiate might spend more time representing their members and less cozying up to politicians, he says. And employees' grievances might get resolved quickly in the workplace, rather than slowly in court.

The metalworkers' proposals could improve matters, at least for big companies. For smaller firms, and foreign investors, the best advice will still be "employer, beware". Ana Rita Gomes, of Mattos Filho Advogados, a São Paulo law firm, talks to potential clients about what she calls "pots of gold": practices that seem innocuous to the uninitiated, but lead straight to the labour courts. One example is stating salaries in a foreign currency. Exchange-rate fluctuations mean that this falls foul of a ban on ever paying an employee less one month than the previous one. Once her clients are suitably terrified, she explains why they should still proceed—with caution. "These difficulties put other investors off," she says. "That means less competition for them, and higher profits."

For smaller firms, and foreign investors, the best advice will still be "employer, beware."

In Pernambuco Mr Lemos is turning his mistakes to good use by advising other businessmen. He tells them to walk away from a deal unless the seller can produce payroll records, settles all outstanding labour-court cases and promises compensation if further cases are brought regarding matters that predate the sale. The new owner will still be liable if the old one cannot pay, he says, but at least there is less scope for bad faith. He recently learned that before his own ill-starred purchase the seller told his staff that the new boss was rich, and that they should save up their grievances until the deal went through.

Brazil Needs Stronger Regulation of Domestic Workers

Ana Virgínia Moreira Gomes and Patrícia Tuma Martins Bertolin

Ana Virgínia Moreira Gomes is a professor of international labor law at the Catholic University of Santos in Brazil; Patrícia Tuma Martins Bertolin is a professor of labor law at Mackenzie Presbyterian University in Brazil. In the following viewpoint, they say that legislation has helped the situation of domestic workers in Brazil. However, they argue, Brazilian domestic workers still face serious problems, including high rates of informal work, discrimination, and violence. The authors conclude that additional efforts must be made to address the particular needs, and protect the labor rights, of domestic workers.

As you read, consider the following questions:

1. According to the authors, what percentage of domestic workers in Brazil are women, what percentage are Afro-Brazilian, and what percentage have, at best, partial education?

2. According to the authors, how do men perceive domestic tasks?

3. What is the origin of discrimination against domestic workers, according to the authors?

Ana Virgínia Moreira Gomes and Patrícia Tuma Martins Bertolin, "Regulatory Challenges of Domestic Work: The Case of Brazil," LLDRL Working Paper Series, No. 3, McGill University, December 2010, pp. 2–16. Reprinted by permission.

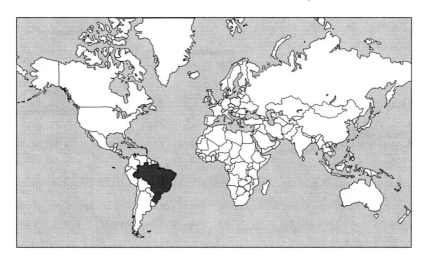

Domestic work, in general, does not receive the same recognition as a "productive" activity as most other forms of work. There are several factors that have contributed to its devaluation. Domestic work is performed at home where conditions are quite different from those found in a typical workplace. Domestic workers work mostly by themselves and are generally isolated from other such workers. Moreover, the economic value of domestic work is harder to assess because there is no commercial output. Even though domestic work has become an economic good, it is still viewed as "women's work", belonging to the household sphere and not to the market.

Disadvantaged Workers

Thus, domestic work's low economic and social status is closely related to the fact that this work is relegated to the most vulnerable groups in society: women, immigrants, disadvantaged racial groups, the uneducated, etc. The Brazilian case is a classic example: Women constitute 94.3% of all domestic workers; 61.8% of them are Afro-Brazilians and 64% have either no education or only partial education at the elementary school level. In 2008, Brazil had 6,600,000 domestic workers, the single largest occupational category in the workforce and the single largest occupation for women.

In recent years, there have been significant improvements in Brazilian law that now recognizes new rights for domestic workers. This process is still not complete, since the law does not guarantee the same rights to domestic workers as it does to other workers. Moreover, domestic workers still bear a heavy cost due to lack of enforcement and frequent violation of their fundamental rights.

The objective of this [viewpoint] is to undertake a critical analysis of Brazilian policy responses to domestic work. The principal argument of the [viewpoint] is that regulatory responses to the problems of domestic workers so far do not address adequately the realities of domestic work, such as the ones related to domestic work itself (for example, isolated workplace) and the ones linked to the profile of domestic workers (for example, that most of them are women). We suggest that not only an adequate policy response is needed but that simply granting domestic workers some of the same rights given to traditional employees will not address their needs fully. Even though the current approach of harmonizing domestic workers' rights with other workers is seen by many as the strongest possible response, we argue in this [viewpoint] that more innovative responses are needed in order to effectively address the specific problems faced by domestic workers. . . .

Domestic work's low economic and social status is closely related to the fact that this work is relegated to the most vulnerable groups in society.

Women and Domestic Work

The vast majority of domestic workers in Brazil are women. Women's participation in the labour market has been problematic due to a patriarchal culture that confined women to the home and made them dependent on the protection and economic support of men. Only since the 1990s has women's participation in the labour market grown more significantly. This increase, however, has often occurred in jobs that offer low wages, require few qualifications and offer very few possibilities for career advancement. Moreover, this increase in labour force participation was often driven by economic needs, and it occurred in spite of prevalent gender discrimination in the labour market.

Since the promulgation of the 1988 federal Constitution, formal discrimination based on gender has been abolished. The 1988 Constitution guarantees the fundamental right of men and women to "have equal rights and obligations" (Article 5, Subparagraph I). Article 7 of the Constitution sets out among the fundamental rights of women workers, a prohibition on discrimination in relation to recruitment and employment on the grounds of sex, age, color or civil status (subparagraph XXX). Nevertheless, gender equality mandated by law has not yet fully transformed the prevailing patriarchal culture that perpetuates gender discrimination more broadly in society and in the labour market in particular.

Within this culture, participation in the labour market did not change the traditional division of domestic tasks, that is, besides having a job, women were still responsible for most of the domestic tasks. Men also did not change their perception of domestic tasks; according to them, this type of work should be done by women and eventually men can agree to help them, but not as an obligation. Women's participation in the labour market has increased without a substantial change in the responsibilities of women at home. A national survey by IBGE [Brazilian Institute of Geography and Statistics] showed that in 2007:

> Only half of men did any domestic tasks (51.4%), while nine out of ten women had this responsibility. For women, having a job did not mean that they would be the only ones

responsible for domestic tasks. On the contrary, when employed, the participation of women in these tasks was even bigger (92%).

In addition, women cannot count on an efficient public system such as an adequate publicly funded day care that would alleviate some of these responsibilities. These developments suggest that women's participation in the labour market is characterized by more precarious work and by their burden of domestic tasks remaining unaltered.

Besides having a job, women were still responsible for most of the domestic tasks.

Due to these characteristics, domestic work is experienced in different ways by women. In order to be able to work while being a mother and taking care of the home, many women in a better economic situation have delegated these tasks to other women with less economic resources, e.g., the domestic workers. These workers often leave home to work in other people's homes and, without any other option, delegate their own domestic tasks to their children. Thus, it is not unusual that an older child would take care of the younger ones. It is also not unusual that this child is a girl who in the future will also become a domestic worker.

On the one hand, middle- and upper-class women are employers and depend on the low cost of domestic work to be able to participate in the labour force. On the other hand, poor and uneducated women seem to have no other option than to work as domestic workers. . . .

Domestic Work and Its Regulation in Brazil

By law, a domestic worker is defined as every person, beyond 18 years, who works on a continuous basis for a person or a family, with no lucrative purpose, within a place of residence.

The most common categories of domestic workers in Brazil are cooks, nannies, cleaners, guards, drivers, gardeners, caregivers, and house managers.

Domestic workers are usually called "domestic employees" (*empregados domésticos*), even though the law differentiates domestic employees from self-employed domestic workers as it guarantees employment rights only to domestic employees. Self-employed domestic workers are called *diaristas* (day workers). In this type of contract, the relationship is not continuous. Usually, labour courts consider that in order for the relationship to be continuous, the worker must work at the employer's house more than three times a week and remuneration must be paid monthly. This [viewpoint] will use the term "domestic worker" to refer to domestic employees. The term "self-employed domestic workers" will refer to domestic workers who are not in an employment relationship. . . .

In 1988, with the promulgation of the new federal Constitution, domestic workers were guaranteed some fundamental labour rights. Article 7 of the 1988 Constitution guarantees to domestic workers ten of the twenty-nine fundamental labour rights guaranteed to all workers: minimum wage; irreducibility of wage; annual bonus equal to one month's salary; paid weekly leave, preferably on Sundays; annual paid vacation with remuneration at least one-third higher than the normal wage; 120 days paid maternity leave; five days paid paternity leave; notice of dismissal; as well as of integration in the social security system.

Since then, the regulation has followed a trend towards the inclusion of domestic workers in the labour and social security systems. More recently, law #11.324/2006 modified some articles of the law #5.859, guaranteeing the right to thirty days of paid vacation, employment protection for pregnant workers, paid legal holidays, and the prohibition of a wage discount in case of supply of meals, housing and hygienic products by the employer. Another important development came with decree #6481 in 2008 that included domestic child labour among the worst forms of child labour and prohibited domestic work for workers under the age of eighteen years. The federal government has also announced that it is preparing a constitutional amendment in order to modify article 7 of the 1988 Constitution (sole paragraph). The constitutional amendment will guarantee domestic workers all fundamental rights in article 7.

In addition to these changes in law, court decisions in their interpretation of the law are also following the trend of equalization of rights between typical workers and domestic workers. As Judge [Maria Cristina] Peduzzi, from the Superior Labour Court, explained:

> Recent legislative changes suggest that there is a historical movement that reveals the normative trend of more equitable rights of domestic workers in relation to rights enjoyed by other employees.

The regulation has followed a trend towards the inclusion of domestic workers in the labour and social security systems.

Challenges Facing the Regulation of Domestic Work

The process of inclusion of domestic workers through the recognition of rights is most welcome and constitutes the first step in achieving full protection for domestic workers. However, some problems do not seem amenable to a change in the law. In other words, the law does not reach some of the most serious violations of domestic workers' rights, such as informality, discrimination and violence against domestic workers. Each of these, intimately connected to the fact that they are mostly women, is discussed in turn.

Informality

In regard to informality, according to the Brazilian Institute of Geography and Statistics (IBGE), the informal sector consists of "economic units owned by self-employed workers or by employers with up to five employees, living in urban areas, regardless of whether this economic unit is the primary or secondary activity of their owners". Even though the IBGE considers domestic workers to be a part of the informal sector, these workers are excluded from the IBGE survey of informality. Instead, the IBGE includes domestic work in their national household survey (PNAD). In this survey, domestic workers are divided into two groups: workers whose labour card (CTPS) is registered with the employer and other workers whose cards are not registered. In 2006 almost two-thirds (65.6 percent) of domestic workers in the six major Brazilian cities did not have their labour card registered with the Ministry of Labour. This somewhat arbitrary exclusion of domestic workers from the informal economy survey results in an underestimation of the number of informal domestic workers. Even those domestic workers who have their labour card registered may have characteristics of informality: not enjoying their labour rights, not contributing to the social security system and not paying income taxes.

Not surprisingly, domestic work is among the activities with low rates of formalization: In 2008, only 25.8 percent of domestic workers had their labour card registered and only 29.3 percent contributed to the social security system. Even though informality has decreased, it has decreased at a rate slower than the rate for other workers. In addition, the low status of domestic workers is also characterized by lower wages. According to the IBGE, "almost one-third of domestic workers receive less than the minimum wage and, among unregistered domestic workers, 40.4% receive less than the minimum wage."

The high informality of domestic work is closely related to poor law enforcement, insufficient labour inspection and the low level of education among domestic workers. Since domestic work is performed inside a private household and many domestic workers have no knowledge of their rights, many of them work informally all their lives. The close relationship that is formed between employer and domestic worker may also contribute to the fact that the number of lawsuits asking for the recognition of an employment relationship is far smaller than the number of informal domestic workers. An effective law reform process cannot afford to ignore these features of the Brazilian labour market.

Since domestic work is performed inside a private household and may domestic workers have no knowledge of their rights, many of them work informally all their lives.

Discrimination

In regard to discrimination, domestic workers are subject not only to direct discrimination, as the law does not grant them the same rights as other workers, but also to indirect discrimination. As pointed out earlier, domestic workers are mostly female, Afro-Brazilian, and hence, among those most susceptible to discrimination. Discrimination based on gender and race is the most common type of discrimination in the Brazilian labour market. In spite of the growing integration of women and Afro-Brazilians into the labour market, the wage disadvantage for these groups is still very pronounced. Although the gap has been narrowing, women still earn less than men in all types of work, including as domestic workers. Further, Afro-Brazilian women are the ones who earn the least. . . .

The history of discrimination against domestic workers can be traced to [the] period of slavery in colonial Brazil. The low social and economic importance of domestic work is one of the vestiges of this era. Domestic work was performed by

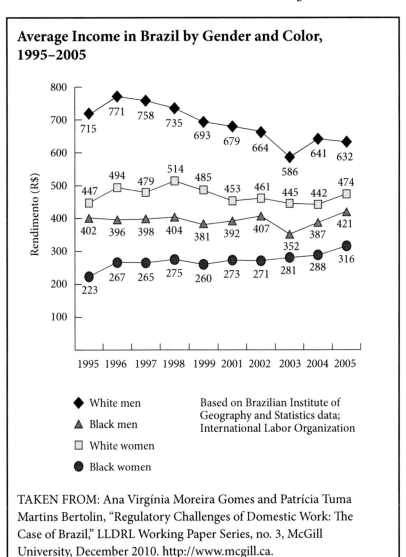

Average Income in Brazil by Gender and Color, 1995–2005

White men

Black men

White women

Black women

Based on Brazilian Institute of Geography and Statistics data; International Labor Organization

TAKEN FROM: Ana Virgínia Moreira Gomes and Patrícia Tuma Martins Bertolin, "Regulatory Challenges of Domestic Work: The Case of Brazil," LLDRL Working Paper Series, no. 3, McGill University, December 2010. http://www.mcgill.ca.

slaves until 1888, when the Áurea law was signed, abolishing slavery without any compensation paid to the ex-slaves. At the time, given that they had no qualification, Afro-Brazilian men went to the labour market accepting any kind of work, and Afro-Brazilian women remained in domestic work, which they were already performing as slaves. Afro-Brazilian women moved from the *senzala* (place where slaves used to live in the farms) to domestic work, in many cases, working for only housing and food, without wages. Since then, racial discrimination has been the main reason that explains why Afro-Brazilian women still constitute the majority of domestic workers. Discrimination explains the relatively worse economic and social conditions Afro-Brazilians face compared to the white population: lower level of education, lower remuneration, living in *favelas* (slums) and exposed to disease and violence. Thus, the combination of low education combined with the need to support their families kept (and continues to keep) these women "trapped" in domestic work.

Brazil has made progress on a number of fronts towards addressing the larger issue of discrimination against women. For example, laws prohibiting discrimination have been enacted. More women are entering the workforce and qualifying for better jobs. Although legislation against discrimination has advanced since the 1988 Constitution, it remains incomplete in addressing gender and colour discrimination in the labour market. Problems faced by Afro-Brazilian women, for example, still remain largely unaddressed.

Women still earn less than men in all types of work, including as domestic workers. Further, Afro-Brazilian women are the ones who earn the least.

Supporting the state's inaction is the idea that Brazil is a "racial democracy", a view which holds that in a mixed race country, race cannot be a factor of discrimination. In this view, the state should not develop policies based on race, because it would be creating racial divisions where they do not exist to begin with. However, the fact that most of the poor population in Brazil is of African descent indicates that race discrimination plays a very important role in the configuration of economic inequality and poverty.

Thus, discrimination against Afro-Brazilian women demands not only the formal prohibition of discrimination, but also affirmative action to promote equal opportunity. For example, the main obstacle that women and Afro-Brazilians face in the labour market is the self-perpetuating unequal opportunity after generations of forced disadvantage. Effective policies cannot be blind to the problems of a domestic worker as a woman and an Afro-Brazilian. Regulation is unlikely to improve their condition unless opportunities are created for access to education and subsequently to better-paid jobs with decent conditions at work.

Violence

In regard to violence against domestic workers, after housewives, these workers are the second biggest group of female victims of domestic violence. The most common cases include moral harassment (for accusation of theft, humiliation), physical aggression, sexual harassment and rape. One example of this type of violence was the case of a domestic worker who was accused of theft and locked in her employers' apartment. The employers left, saying that they would call the police. Left alone and locked in the apartment, the worker fell from the apartment and died, perhaps in an attempt to escape or commit suicide.

Sexual harassment is possibly the most common form of violence against domestic workers. The fear to be fired makes many workers afraid to denounce the aggressor or even worse, to submit themselves to the harassment. The practice is so common that some families will not allow their young daughters to work as domestic workers as they are afraid of the employer's behavior. While the recognition of employment rights for domestic workers has become a part of the political debate, the problem of violence against domestic workers is not yet a part of this debate.

In India, More Flexible Labor Regulations Are Needed to Encourage Growth

Sadiq Ahmed and Shantayanan Devarajan

Sadiq Ahmed is a Bangladeshi national and senior manager for regional programs in the South Asia region for World Bank. Shantayanan Devarajan is World Bank's chief economist for South Asia. In the following viewpoint, the authors write that India is experiencing promising growth. However, they argue, the manufacturing sector is not growing as rapidly as it should. The authors say that the sector has been constrained by a system of rigid and confusing labor laws. They conclude that labor regulation reform is necessary to spur manufacturing growth.

As you read, consider the following questions:

1. What good news about economic growth do the authors provide?

2. According to the authors, how does the informal manufacturing sector in Korea compare to the informal manufacturing sector in India?

3. What are SEZs, and why do the authors say they may be of limited use to India in spurring growth?

Sadiq Ahmed and Shantayanan Devarajan, "Labor Laws: To Create Good Jobs, Reform Labor Regulations," World Bank, February 20, 2007. The World Bank: The World Bank authorizes the use of this material subject to the terms and conditions on its website, http://www.worldbank.org/terms. Reprinted by permission.

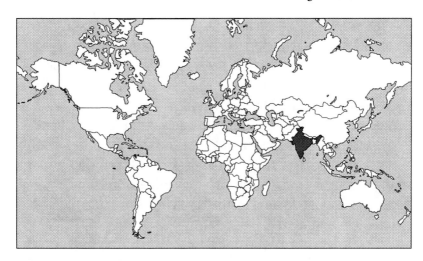

India has been remarkably successful in boosting economic growth: Its economy has grown at about 6 percent per annum since the 1990s, with growth accelerating to 9 percent over the past two years. Absolute poverty has been cut in half, and the country seems set to achieve middle income status soon.

The Informal Economy

Among all this good news, some puzzles remain. Despite recent growth, India's manufacturing sector still accounts for less than 15 percent of GDP [gross domestic product] and employs less than 15 percent of the workforce. This is in stark contrast to the fast-growing East Asian countries such as Korea, China and Thailand where rapid expansion in manufacturing has generated large-scale employment that has lifted millions out of poverty.

For most Indians, especially the poor and marginalized, labor is the principal asset. If India is to sustain its current levels of growth and reduce poverty, it has to provide jobs with good wages for the vast majority of its people, as well as for the 80 million new entrants who are expected to join the workforce over the next decade.

Yet most manufacturing jobs in India are in the informal sector which is characterized by low productivity and wages and to which labor laws do not apply. This is disproportionately large compared to East Asia: In India, small informal firms employ a sizeable 40 percent of the country's workers compared with only 4 percent in Korea. On the other hand in 2003, India's organized manufacturing sector employed only about 1.3 percent of the total labor force of over 450 million, most of it in the private sector. Even more unfortunately, employment in the formal manufacturing sector declined between 1996 and 2002.

What is preventing manufacturing in India from becoming the engine for mass employment it has been in East Asia? Take the textiles and clothing sector which accounts for a fifth of India's exports. It employs almost 10 percent of India's workforce, or some 35 million people, and has the potential to add another 12 million new jobs—dwarfing the 1–2 million jobs created by the much-heralded IT [information technology] and BPO [business process outsourcing—that is, performing services for countries overseas, such as call center technical support] sector. The sector was expected to boom after the multi-fiber agreement was abolished in 2005. While in the first year of quota-free exports, textiles and clothing exports jumped 23 percent, similar to China's, growth slowed to about 10–12 percent the following year (2006). Not only was this slower than China, it was also slower than Bangladesh, Pakistan, and Vietnam.

Most manufacturing jobs in India are in the informal sector which is characterized by low productivity and wages and to which labor laws do not apply.

Constraints on Manufacturing

The sector is clearly facing constraints that are hindering its expansion. China's remarkable success—with exports of 20 billion finished garments or roughly 4 for every person in the world—has largely been explained by its state-of-the-art factories and efficient transport infrastructure. While huge infrastructure bottlenecks have undoubtedly kept India's textile and clothing industry small and fragmented, what is perhaps less well known is how India's archaic labor regulations are hurting the sector's growth.

Anecdotal evidence suggests that Indian manufacturers often set up several plants instead of a single large one to get around labor laws. This, however, limits their flexibility to meet seasonal variations in demand. They also lose out on economies of scale and investment: On average, Indian textile and clothing firms have only 10–20 percent of the machines that a typical Chinese plant does.

Of course, labor laws are needed. Workers need protection. But labor laws should protect workers, not jobs. In India, current regulations end up doing more harm than good. In international comparisons, India stands out as having one of the most rigid labor laws in the world. A recent study estimated that in 1997, India could have had more than 1 million more jobs in the textiles and clothing sector alone if its labor regulations had been less restrictive. Overall the country could have had 2.8 million more good quality formal sector jobs—a startling 45 percent of existing employment in the organized manufacturing sector on that date.

Not all of these losses are due to the difficulty of retrenching workers: More than half are a result of the complexity of laws and the difficulty of resolving disputes. There are currently 47 central laws and 157 state regulations that directly affect labor markets. These are often inconsistent and at times overlapping. It is impossible for either firms or workers to be aware of their rights and obligations when rules and regulations are spread over such numerous national and state level acts.

It is clearly possible to do much better. Active labor market programs and policies (ALMPs), as recommended by the International Labour Organization and other bodies internationally, are starting in India and may need to be strengthened. ALMPs can be subdivided broadly into three categories: direct job creation, labor market training, and job brokerage (improving the match between job seekers and vacancies). For now, the rural employment guarantee program is an important start. If implemented well, it promises to provide an important form of job security for the rural labor force. More is possible and could include effective information and employment exchanges, social insurance mechanisms for informal sector workers, and strengthened technical and vocational education programs. Amending the plethora of existing labor regulations is itself an integral part of the job-creating ALMP strategy for India.

In India, current regulations end up doing more harm than good.

Special Economic Zones

The Government of India has been seeking to spur manufacturing growth by setting up special economic zones (SEZs). Although the program has been put on hold till the land acquisition and social safety net issues for rural landowners have been resolved, it is important to note that the international experience on SEZs is mixed. Tax packages alone are often not enough to attract investment. Moreover, they are often costly. Their role in employment generation is usually marginal. SEZs may be useful in testing new approaches, in policy as well as governance structures. They can be catalysts for reforms as the China case suggests. But SEZs cannot be a shortcut to development, and should not detract from the overall reform effort in India.

An improvement in labor regulations, perhaps spurred at individual state level within a central enabling framework, will provide an opportunity to accelerate manufacturing growth and especially employment in key labor-intensive sectors, including the crucial textiles and clothing sector, within the next decade [2007–2017].

Chile Must Adopt Stronger Workplace Safety Regulations for Mines

Daniela Estrada

Daniela Estrada is a Chilean correspondent for Inter Press Service news agency. In the following viewpoint, she reports on the rescue of Chilean miners trapped underground for more than two months in 2010. Estrada provides quotes that suggest that the miners were the victims of systematic safety failures caused by poor working conditions in Chilean mines. She notes that the government has portrayed the miners as heroes, but suggests that what is really needed is not individual heroism but reform of safety conditions. She also says that workers should have more of a voice in mine regulation.

As you read, consider the following questions:

1. According to Estrada, how many workplace accidents and deaths were there in Chile in 2009?

2. Why does Kirsten Sehnbruch say that Chile has come off well following the mine disaster?

3. What does María Ester Feres say is the problem with trends like outsourcing?

Daniela Estrada, "Chilean Miners Rescue May Mark a Watershed in Workplace Safety," IPS, October 13, 2010. Reprinted by permission.

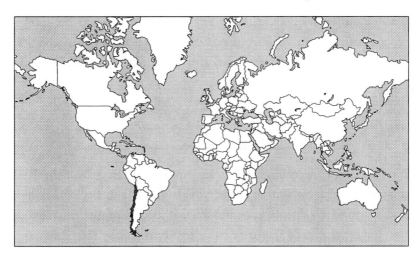

"This country has to understand that changes must be made," said Mario Sepulveda, the second Chilean miner—of the group of 33 trapped 700 metres underground for over two months—rescued in the early hours of Wednesday morning [October 2010].

Many Workplace Accidents

But what changes? What lessons has the mining accident in the northern region of Atacama left Chile, the world's largest producer of copper?

In the media frenzy surrounding the rescue operation that started Tuesday night, no one has bothered to mention that there were more than 191,000 workplace accidents in this South American country of 17 million people in 2009, including 443 deaths, and 155 deaths in the first quarter of this year alone.

"The miners are not heroes," as they have been called around the world for surviving underground for over two months; "they are victims," Néstor Jorquera, president of the CONFEMIN mining union, told IPS.

"After our compañeros are rescued, we're going to do everything we can to hold the people who were responsible for this accountable," said the leader of CONFEMIN, which represents more than 18,000 miners who work at small, medium-size and large privately owned mines—including the 33 miners at the San José mine in Copiapó, Atacama.

"The miners are not heroes . . . they are victims."

In an unprecedented rescue operation that has thrilled television viewers around the world while it is broadcast live and covered by hundreds of Chilean and foreign journalists, the government of right-wing President Sebastián Piñera is bringing up the 32 Chileans and one Bolivian trapped in the mine since an Aug. 5 collapse.

The first miner, Florencio Avalos, came up in the capsule named Phoenix after midnight and was welcomed by the rescuers and by Piñera and several cabinet ministers. By the time this [viewpoint] came out, 16 miners had been rescued, and the last miner may be brought up earlier than expected, by Wednesday night.

Critics say Camp Hope, where relatives of the miners have been staying near the mine, has turned into the set of a reality show where the private lives of the miners and their families and the details of the spectacular rescue have trumped concerns about the poor safety conditions that caused the accident.

Television programmes that plan to follow the rescued San Esteban mining company workers over the next few months have already been announced, as well as books and films about their ordeal.

There has also been criticism of the government for making political mileage out of the case, given Piñera's continuous presence at the mine and his frequent references to the strength of the miners in his speeches, as symbols "of the Chilean spirit of struggle against adversity."

In the eyes of the world, "Chile has come off very well because of the rescue effort, and the responsibility assumed by the state," Kirsten Sehnbruch, a professor at the University of Chile's Institute of Public Affairs, told IPS [Inter Press Service]. But at the same time, the accident "has caused tremendous damage to the country's image, because everyone is wondering why it happened."

The Result of Negligence

She said the accident was the result of negligence on the part of both the mining company and the government.

According to Sehnbruch, "in any developed country, the owners of the mine would be in jail."

The two Chileans who own the mine located in the desert 800 km north of the capital are facing criminal charges for serious bodily injury in connection with an earlier accident, in which a miner lost a leg. They are under court order not to leave the country.

"In any developed country, the owners of the mine would be in jail."

"The joy over the near epic rescue that has been the result of the strength and wisdom of the miners of Atacama makes it necessary for us not to forget that situations like this one are absolutely avoidable," María Ester Feres, director of the private Central University of Chile's centre on labour relations, research and advice, told IPS.

Feres pointed out that "last year alone, according to partial figures (provided by companies affiliated with private insurance providers), more than 191,000 work-related accidents were counted" in this country.

In a speech after the first miner was rescued, Piñera said "we are carrying out a complete review of safety standards," not only in the mining industry but in other sectors as well.

Conditions at the San José Mine in Chile, Site of the 2010 Mine Collapse

The men entering the San José mine worked not at the safe modern mines but instead belonged to the most risky sub-culture of this entire industry—low-tech, rustic miners known locally as "Los Pirquineros." While the classic Chilean pirquinero had equipment no more sophisticated than a donkey and a pickax, the men at the San José mine called themselves "mechanized *pirquineros*," meaning they operated modern machinery inside the rickety infrastructure of a classically dangerous operation. Unlike other mines that had rats and insects, the San José mine was sterile—except for the occasional scorpion. Inside the mine, the daily routine was akin to the lifestyle of a California forty-niner searching for gold in the days of Abraham Lincoln. These miners were regularly crushed—"ironed flat" in local lingo—by thousand-pound blocks of rock that unlatched from the roof with terrifying regularity. The rocks inside the San José mine were so sharp that the miners knew that even brushing up against the wall was like scraping a razor across their skin.

Jonathan Franklin,
33 Men: Inside the Miraculous Survival
and Dramatic Rescue of the Chilean Miners.
New York: G.P. Putnam's Sons, 2011.

A National Policy Is Needed

According to Feres, Chile does not have "coherent, efficient public policies or a national structure in the area of work safety and health."

"To judge by what is happening in agribusiness, salmon farming, the ports, construction and other industries, it is clear that decent work is not a strategic objective of this country's model for economic growth," the expert said.

The problems include long workdays, insufficient breaks, low pay, high turnover, and high levels of informal employment, she said.

A commission set up in August by Piñera is drafting a report on workplace safety, to be delivered on Nov. 22.

The president also announced the creation of a mining superintendency to regulate and enforce safety standards, a restructuring of the National Geology and Mining Service, increased funds for inspections, and the establishment of another advisory committee, to review mining safety regulations.

Mining unions complain that the government has gone after the weakest link, closing down small, dangerous mines that operate on a semi-informal basis in Atacama.

CONFEMIN president Jorquera called for the ratification of International Labour Organization (ILO) Convention 176 on safety and health in mines, which was adopted in 1995 and went into force in 1998. But he complained that "the government isn't interested in this, because it believes it won't solve the problem."

Feres said "the government's actions are not pointing in the right direction," because it set up "a commission that is only focused on labour safety, without including an analysis of overall working conditions in its objectives." Nor did it include labour unions and other key actors, she added.

She also criticised the business community's attempt to blame the problem "only on small companies."

Mining unions complain that the government has gone after the weakest link, closing down small, dangerous mines that operate on a semi-informal basis in Atacama, without offering any support to help them improve conditions.

Although CONFEMIN and the Central Workers Union (CUT)—Chile's largest trade union—will deliver a petition to the government, and other unions are organising as well, Jorquera is not optimistic with regard to the prospect of significant changes in working conditions, because of deeper underlying problems like outsourcing.

In addition, trends like outsourcing "externalise labour costs and risks, and fragment and hinder the labour movement and the organized participation of workers in setting and overseeing working conditions," said Feres.

"Tackling labour problems as a key dimension of economic and social development, and workplace safety and health as a state policy, with a national structure and an integral and participative focus is an urgent challenge, in order to make the leap to true social and economic development," she added.

For his part, Jorquera said the "business community's regrettable irresponsibility" has provided "a great opportunity" for workers "to protest and reveal everything that is hidden in this country," now that the eyes of the world are on Chile.

In Greece, Vacation and Retirement Provisions Are Too Generous

Spiegel Online

Spiegel Online *is the electronic version of the German newspaper* Spiegel. *In the following viewpoint, the paper reports on a statement by German chancellor Angela Merkel, in which she argues that Greece's retirement age and pensions are too generous. According to Merkel, Germany will only help Greece out of its economic crisis if workers' rights are scaled back.* Spiegel Online *notes that the remarks caused controversy, with some expressing doubt as to whether Germany should continue to aid Greece and opposition politicians criticizing Merkel for attacking Greece to win popular applause in Germany.*

As you read, consider the following questions:

1. What differences does the author describe between the retirement age in Greece and the retirement age in Germany?
2. How is Greece planning to raise fifty billion euros in assets, according to the viewpoint?
3. What did Green Party officials say about Merkel's comments, as reported in the viewpoint?

Spiegel Online, "Merkel Blasts Greece over Retirement Age, Vacation," May 18, 2011. Reprinted by permission.

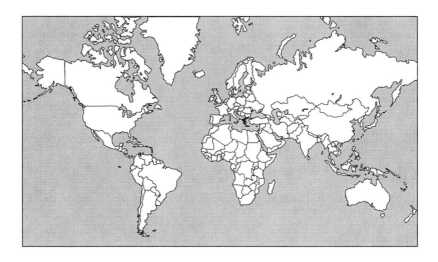

It was the kind of criticism that one isn't used to hearing from Angela Merkel. Normally sober and analytical to a fault, the German chancellor on Tuesday [May 2011] evening blasted a handful of heavily indebted southern European countries, saying they needed to raise retirement ages and reduce vacation days.

Coordinating Retirement Age

Keeping debt under control, Merkel said in a speech at an event held by her party, the conservative Christian Democratic Union, in the western German town of Meschede, isn't the only priority. "It is also important that people in countries like Greece, Spain and Portugal are not able to retire earlier than in Germany—that everyone exerts themselves more or less equally. That is important."

She added: "We can't have a common currency [the euro] where some get lots of vacation time and others very little. That won't work in the long term."

There are indeed significant differences between retirement ages in the two countries. Greece announced reforms to its pension system in early 2010 aimed at reducing early retirement and raising the average age of retirement to 63. Incentives to keep workers in the labor market beyond 65 have likewise been adopted. Germany voted in 2007 to raise the retirement age from 65 to 67 over the next several years.

"We can't have a common currency where some get lots of vacation time and others very little. That won't work in the long term."

In January of this year [2011], Merkel proposed a "pact for competitiveness" that would force EU [European Union] members to coordinate their national policies on issues like tax, wages and retirement ages. A watered-down version of the pact was agreed upon at a summit in March.

Merkel's broadside comes at a time when doubts are rising in Europe as to the efficacy of bailout packages put together for euro-zone countries struggling under mountains of debt. Attention in recent weeks, however, has focused once again on Greece as it has become clear that, despite €110 billion ($157 billion) in aid granted to the country in 2010, Athens may need more.

On Tuesday, following two days of meetings to address Greece's plight, top euro-zone officials for the first time indicated that some sort of debt restructuring may be in store for Athens after all. The European Union had been adamant in its refusal to consider a partial Greek default for fear that it could destabilize the markets. But on Tuesday, Jean-Claude Juncker, who heads up the Euro group—made up of the finance ministers of the 17 euro-zone member states—said that a so-called "soft restructuring of Greek debt" may be possible.

European Commissioner for Economic and [Financial] Affairs Olli Rehn seconded the idea, saying "a voluntary extension of loan maturities, a so-called re-profiling or rescheduling on a voluntary basis, could be examined."

A prerequisite for such a move, Juncker said, was that Greece raise €50 billion through the privatization of state-

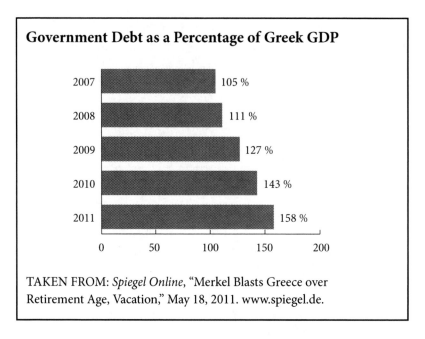

Government Debt as a Percentage of Greek GDP

Year	Percentage
2007	105 %
2008	111 %
2009	127 %
2010	143 %
2011	158 %

TAKEN FROM: *Spiegel Online*, "Merkel Blasts Greece over Retirement Age, Vacation," May 18, 2011. www.spiegel.de.

owned assets. He said he expects that at least €15 billion in assets to be sold this year. Greek Prime Minister George Papandreou said that an aggressive privatization strategy could cut his country's debt—currently at 150 percent of Greek gross domestic product—by 20 percentage points.

Intended for a Domestic Audience

Merkel's sharp tone on Tuesday evening was almost certainly intended primarily for a domestic audience. Her junior coalition partner, the business-friendly Free Democrats, has been vocally skeptical of additional euro-zone bailout packages, even though they voted in favor of the European Stability Mechanism—a permanent euro backstop set to enter force in 2013—at a weekend party convention. And the Christian Social Union (CSU), the Bavarian sister party to Merkel's Christian Democrats, is considering polling its members on whether it should support an additional aid package for Greece.

"The lesson from Greece is that despite the euro rescue scheme, it is in no better a position today than a year ago," Alexander Dobrindt, the CSU's general secretary, told the Munich-based paper *Münchner Merkur*. "Our members have to be consulted on such a basic question as whether we should tolerate a different Europe."

Others among Merkel's conservatives have also voiced resistance to the European Stability Mechanism, making it possible that she will have to rely on votes from the opposition in the German parliament, which will vote on the euro backstop in the autumn.

Such concerns, it would seem, were not far from Merkel's mind as she spoke on Tuesday evening. "Of course we want the euro and of course we don't want to see that a country goes broke, so to speak, and that we all then follow," she said. "But we can't just show solidarity and then say that these countries can continue as before."

"Yes, Germany will help. But Germany only helps when the others exert themselves as well. And that exertion must be demonstrated."

Among Germany's opposition, however, Merkel's comments were not at all well received. "Ms. Merkel is once again opting for populism over substantive arguments," opposition Social Democrat leader Sigmar Gabriel told *Spiegel Online*. "It is shameful that Merkel is gambling away the European idea . . . only to receive praise from the tabloids. She is fomenting anti-European resentment."

"Yes, Germany will help. But Germany only helps when the others exert themselves as well."

The Greens were equally scathing in their critique of Merkel. Green Party co-head Cem Özdemir told *Spiegel Online* that Merkel's "arbitrary selection of specific issues doesn't help countries like Greece, Portugal and Spain nor does it reflect reality."

Daniel Cohn-Bendit, head of the Greens in European Parliament, called Merkel's comments "absurd." "Of course people in southern Europe work a lot," he said. Instead of "looking for cheap applause," Merkel should make concrete proposals, he added.

American Vacation Policy Is Not Sufficiently Generous

David Moberg

David Moberg is a senior editor at In These Times. *In the following viewpoint, Moberg argues that Americans receive far less vacation and far fewer sick days than do Europeans. He says that this is the result of political differences; unions in Europe are stronger, and there are political parties that side with workers rather than with corporations. He says that Americans would be healthier and happier with more time off and that America can afford more time off. Instead, he says, excess wealth has been funneled to the wealthiest people in society, and American workers suffer.*

As you read, consider the following questions:

1. According to Moberg, how much vacation do full-time workers in Europe take on average?
2. When and why did paid leave in America and Europe diverge, according to Moberg?
3. What is the Take Back Your Time campaign, and for what policy changes is it pushing?

Last year Mary Lou Eckart took her first vacation in five years, a trip from her home in Decatur, Ill., to see her grandchildren in Florida. But the Illinois state government,

David Moberg, "What Vacation Days?," *In These Times*, June 18, 2007. Reprinted by permission.

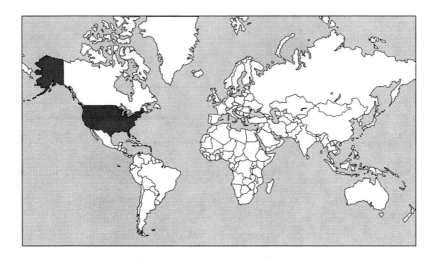

which pays her to care for a severely disabled teenage girl, provides her no paid vacation time. So Eckart took the girl—and her work—with her.

No Sick Leave

She faces a similar bind if she gets sick. "I just had an incident two weeks ago," she says. "I had an inner ear infection that I didn't know about, and I passed out. My 17-year-old daughter covered for me while I recovered. I get no paid vacation, no time off, no sick leave. But if they put these clients in a nursing home, I know that is very expensive. I'd love to have a vacation. I'd love to be able to get away. I'd love to have someone fill in for me. I feel like we deserve more than what we're getting."

Eckart's story is all too common: Nearly one-fourth of American workers have no paid vacation or holidays, according to a recent study from the D.C.-based Center for Economic and Policy Research (CEPR), and nearly half of all private sector workers have no paid sick days. But if Eckart were living in any other industrialized country, she would be legally guaranteed at least two weeks paid vacation and—in 136 countries—from seven to more than 30 paid sick days. The United

States is the only rich country that does not mandate paid vacations and paid sick days, and Americans who are afforded such benefits enjoy far less time off than workers in other wealthy nations.

Americans now work more every year, on average, than workers in any other industrialized country (except for a virtual tie with New Zealand). With women working longer hours each year, the average annual work time for a married couple is growing steadily, and family time—including the crucial bonding experience of vacations—has suffered. Full-time workers in much of Europe typically take seven to eight weeks of vacation and holidays each year—that's double the American average for full-time workers. Overall, the average private sector worker in the United States gets about nine paid vacation days and six paid holidays each year. Low-paid, part-time or small-business workers typically get far fewer, sometimes none. The same holds for paid sick leave: 72 percent of the highest-paid quarter of private sector workers get paid sick days compared to only 21 percent of workers in the lowest-paid quarter.

Nearly one-fourth of American workers have no paid vacation or holidays.

Intercontinental Disparity

Why do workers in other rich countries have more paid time off? Mainly because laws demand employers provide it. The European Union requires its members to set a minimum standard of four weeks paid vacation (covering part-time workers as well). Finland and France require six weeks paid vacation, plus additional paid holidays. Most countries require workers to take the time off and employers to give them vacation at convenient times. Some governments even require employers to pay bonuses so workers can afford to do more than sit at home on vacation. On top of that, unions in Europe and other rich industrialized countries—whose contracts cover up to 90 percent of the workforce—typically negotiate additional time off. Meanwhile, the standard work week is slightly shorter in many European countries, and workers retire earlier with better public pensions.

Until the early '70s, European and American workers logged similar hours. But the pattern then drastically diverged, with Europeans getting more vacation time, around the same time that U.S. income inequality began growing. In the United States, corporations gained the upper hand against workers and their declining unions, and the Democratic Party started shifting away from working-class concerns. In Europe, stronger unions and left political parties pushed for shorter work hours. In some cases, as jobs were lost when traditional industries restructured or work was outsourced, unions saw reduced work time as a way to share work. But more often, unions were continuing the battle to share wealth in the form of more leisure, which had started a century earlier with the movement for an eight-hour day—the goal of Chicago protestors in May, 1886, that ended in the Haymarket massacre, repression of the labor movement, and creation of May 1 as the international workers' holiday.

The difference in work hours between the United States and most industrial countries "is exactly a manifestation of the same forces driving broader inequality," says CEPR economist John Schmitt, pointing to deterioration of the minimum wage, pensions, public services, health insurance and wages under pressure from globalization, deregulation, privatization and attacks on unions. "Workers haven't been able to translate higher productivity gains into higher pay or benefits, and they've been unable to address the time crunch."

"People in the United States don't even understand what could be possible on this issue [of paid time off]," Schmitt says. "This is one of the most important ideological victories of the right in the last 30 years—to persuade us we aren't rich enough to treat workers well. We're incredibly rich, getting richer every year, and we have plenty of resources to pay adequate wages, pensions, health insurance and vacations, but we've chosen to give that money to the top five percent."

European and other industrialized countries have divided their growing ability to produce differently. For example, Europe has nearly caught up with—and many countries have pulled ahead of—the United States in labor productivity (the output from each hour of work), the key measure of an economy's potential.

Why do workers in other rich countries have more paid time off? Mainly because laws demand employers provide it.

In recent years, however, American workers have rapidly increased the amount of goods and services they produce each year, in comparison to Europe. These two measurements have largely diverged because Europeans have been enjoying more time away from the job, just as they've been enjoying a more egalitarian society.

According to Harvard economist Alberto Alesina, Europeans are happier, and have less stress and insecurity, which is good for health and longevity. Studies in the United States, for example, indicate that taking vacations cuts in half the risk of heart attacks for men. Longer, mandated vacations haven't undercut the competitiveness of other rich countries, and there's evidence that they increase labor productivity.

Plus, recent increases in the U.S. gross domestic product haven't significantly helped most Americans: The super-rich have captured most of the income gains. An accurate calculation of the gross domestic product—subtracting such costs as crime, environmental depredations, militarism and declining social trust—would actually show that growth in economic output has brought few, if any, real gains in welfare for American society. Indeed, CEPR economists David Rosnick and Mark Weisbrot argue that Europe's shorter work hours help the environment by reducing energy consumption and carbon emissions.

Taking Back Time

Most Americans would be better off with more paid vacation and leave, but inequality, insecurity and the competitive rat race drive people to work even harder, often just to keep their heads above water. It's very difficult for individuals to demand more time, even if the limited polling available suggests it would be popular. Major gains will only come from an organized movement and changed laws. One organization, Take Back Your Time, founded by writer and documentary filmmaker John de Graaf, is trying to persuade presidential candidates to support its proposal for mandating three weeks of paid vacation for all workers. "I think the political figure who would pick up on this issue would find great resonance," de Graaf says, but so far nobody has.

At this point, more modest proposals have a better chance to succeed. Sen. Ted Kennedy (D-Mass.) and Rep. Rosa De-Lauro (D-Conn.) have introduced the Healthy Families Act, which would guarantee seven days of paid leave for all workers to deal with their own or a family member's illness. Beyond the obvious help to the individuals who need care, such legislation would help businesses economically. Rather than putting in an unproductive day at work spreading communicable diseases (or sending their sick child to spread illness at a child care center), workers could just stay at home, and it would reduce the employee turnover that results from workers taking off unauthorized, unpaid sick days. Five states have mandatory temporary disability insurance programs to cover income losses from short illnesses, and last November [2006], San Francisco voters approved the first mandated paid sick days in the United States. The Working Families Party in New

York is now campaigning for paid leave for new parents and adults caring for ailing relatives, a protection California passed in 2004 (thus strengthening the unpaid family and medical leave federal law provides).

Most Americans would be better off with more paid vacation and leave, but inequality, insecurity and the competitive rat race drive people to work even harder, often just to keep their heads above water.

Mandated paid sick days would help workers like Elnora Collins, a home care worker in Chicago. "If you get sick, you go to work sick. If you show up for work, you endanger your patients. If you don't show up for work, you get no pay. I recently lost a whole day's pay, because I ended up in a hospital for an overnight stay. It was an anxiety attack, like a heart attack. It's very frightening. And then, when you look at that paycheck, you really cry."

Compare the work time and leisure in the United States to that in other rich countries, and we all have good reason to share in her tears.

Periodical and Internet Sources Bibliography

The following articles have been selected to supplement the diverse views presented in this chapter.

Mohammad Amin	"Labor Regulation and Employment in India's Retail Stores," *Journal of Comparative Economics*, vol. 37, no. 1, 2009.
Associated Press	"Greece's Early Retirement Rules Breed Resentment," *USA Today*, May 18, 2010.
BBC News	"Greece Plans to Ban Early Retirement," February 9, 2010. http://news.bbc.co.uk.
Steven Bodzin	"Chile Mine Collapse Sounds Alarm on Safety Standards," *Christian Science Monitor*, August 24, 2010.
Economist	"Brazil's Strange Labour Market: On Steroids?," March 10, 2011.
Economist	"Heavy Going: The Biggest Enemy of Brazil's Promise Is an Overbearing State," April 12, 2007.
Andrew Hammel	"Vacation Policies in Europe and the USA," *German Joys* (blog), May 18, 2007. http://andrewhammel.typepad.com.
HR Unplugged (blog)	"Vacation Time—America vs. Europe," July 14, 2010. http://hrunplugged.wordpress.com.
Elisabeth Rosenthal	"For Every Rescued Miner in Chile, Hundreds Far Less Lucky," *Green* (blog), October 14, 2010. http://green.blogs.nytimes.com.
Ian Traynor	"Angela Merkel Dashes Greek Hopes of Rescue Bid," *Guardian*, February 11, 2010.
United Nations	"The Story of Creuza Oliveira," April 2009. www.ohchr.org.

CHAPTER 2

Unions and Collective Bargaining

China Needs Collective Bargaining to Protect Workers' Rights

Han Dongfang

Han Dongfang is the director of China Labour Bulletin. In the following viewpoint, he argues that China's workers need collective bargaining rights to reduce hours and increase wages. Stronger collective bargaining, he says, would also reduce the risk and intensity of labor disputes. Dongfang hopes that a 2008 labor law in China will open the way for collective bargaining. He also hopes it will encourage Chinese trade unions to throw off management control and become genuinely representative of workers.

As you read, consider the following questions:

1. According to Dongfang, why do employers routinely pay the minimum wage mandated by law?
2. Why do Chinese workers often opt to work longer hours, according to Dongfang?
3. According to Dongfang, why is the Labor Contract Law timely?

The *Labor Contract Law* that took effect on 1 January 2008 and has been much publicized by local governments across China would appear to provide a further legal guarantee of

Han Dongfang, "Collective Bargaining and the New Labour Contract Law," *China Labour Bulletin*, February 26, 2008. Reprinted by permission.

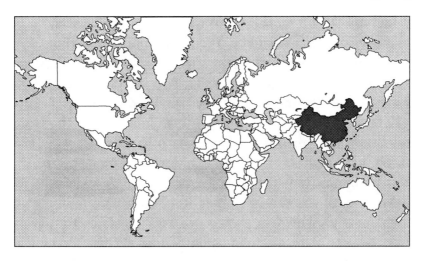

workers' rights in China. In fact, in recent years the Chinese government has introduced a series of laws and regulations to protect the rights and interests of workers, including the *Trade Union Law* in 1992, the *Labor Law* in 1995, the *Production Safety Law* in 2002 and the *Provisions on Collective Contract* in 2004. From a strictly legal standpoint, it would be fair to say that the protection of workers' rights in China is systematically improving. But in China's factories, serious violations of the rights and interests of workers are increasingly common. Unless the causes for this embarrassing situation are addressed and effective remedial action is taken, no amount of legislation is going [to] bring about a fundamental improvement in China's labour rights.

Minimum Wage by Default

The reason China's labour rights situation is going from bad to worse despite more legislation is not hard to find. Put simply, workers in China still do not have the right to collective bargaining.

Although the law stipulates a minimum wage, the only way for an enterprise to determine a reasonable wage, work hours and working conditions based on the legally mandated minimum wage and the enterprise's actual business and operational situation would be through genuine negotiations between management and labour. Yet because Chinese workers lack the right to engage in collective bargaining, employers routinely pay the minimum wage mandated by law to all employees as if it were a reasonable wage in all cases. The basic minimum wage mandated by law was originally meant to be a minimum standard, but in the vast majority of enterprises this minimum wage has become the basic flat wage paid by default to all workers. In other words, the minimum wage regulations designed to protect workers' rights and interests have become the legal foundation of management's exploitation of labour.

Workers in China still do not have the right to collective bargaining.

The *Labor Law* also sets strict limits on work hours and overtime, but the excessively low piece-rate wages paid by employers make it impossible for workers to earn a living wage by working eight hours a day. Because they cannot bargain collectively, individual employees naturally dare not to ask for a piece-rate rise on their own, so their only option is . . . to work longer hours. In most places where employees work excessively long hours, it turns out that they have asked to do so themselves, and as such, the local labour bureaus—who are supposed to monitor and address breaches of work hour regulations—are powerless to intervene in this "reasonable" violation of the law.

Low Wages, Long Hours

An effective collective bargaining system would offer China's workers a quick way out of the dead end of excessively low wages and long hours they currently find themselves in. It would also serve a political and social "fireproofing" function

The All-China Federation of Trade Unions (ACFTU)

The ACFTU is the largest self-professed and legally mandated organisation to represent labour in the world, with more 'members' than all other trade unions in the world combined. By the end of September 2006 there were 31 provincial trade union federations, ten national industrial unions and 1.3 million grassroots trade union organisations (in 2.8 million enterprises and institutions) affiliated to the ACFTU. The membership of the ACFTU totals 169.9 million.... Overall union membership is 73.6 per cent of registered workers in China, and this is serviced by 543,000 full-time trade union officials and 4.6 million part-time cadres.

Despite its mammoth size, the ACFTU today is usually dismissed either internationally as a sham union or domestically as ineffectual or irrelevant. Nevertheless, its sheer size creates a major potential force for change within China and the international industrial relations scene in general. This ... is the story of how the labour movement within China was organized into this single institution, and the dynamics of a state organ caught between worker aspirations and state requirements. The result has been an organ that has oftentimes been seen as serving neither national nor worker interests. In practice radical elements within both the state and among workers have pushed the ACFTU into actions oscillating between workers' representative, state stooge and complete irrelevance.

Bill Taylor and Qi Li,
"The ACFTU's Changing Role in China's Tumultuous
Social Development," in Trade Unionism Since 1945—
Towards a Global History, Volume 2:
The Americas, Asia and Australia, *ed. Craig Phelan.*
Oxford: Peter Lang, 2009.

in that it would reduce the risk of labour disputes sparking conflagrations that can only be put out after the damage has already been done. Collective bargaining would be a proactive, preventive rather than a passive after-the-fact method of protecting the rights and interests of workers.

I think that as far as establishing a collective bargaining system is concerned, there is no doubt that the new *Labor Contract Law* is timely and well positioned within China's legislative landscape. It is timely because after three decades of growing tension between labour and management, both the Chinese Communist leadership and ordinary people from all walks of life agree that something needs to be done to prevent the situation from escalating into a disaster. The law is well positioned because it effectively builds on the labour rights and labour dispute laws and regulations that have been passed in recent years and provides the necessary legal basis for a genuine collective bargaining system. In particular, the *Labor Contract Law* stipulates that it is the employer's responsibility to sign a collective labour contract with the employees' representative within an enterprise.

An effective collective bargaining system would offer China's workers a quick way out of the dead end of excessively low wages and long hours they currently find themselves in.

For years, tension between labour and management has built up while China's trade unions have been content to go through the motions of representing the interests of workers. But if the All-China Federation of Trade Unions (ACFTU) and its branch unions grasp the opportunity presented by the *Labor Contract Law* at this key juncture, I believe that after a couple of years of finding their way and gaining experience, the unions ought to be able to create a genuine and effective collective bargaining system in China.

In addition, a well-designed collective bargaining system would also lay the foundations for grassroots unions. Right now, the vast majority of "trade unions" in enterprises are controlled by the management. They do not speak for workers and, in fact, do not even listen to the higher-level unions that are supposed to supervise them. Thus, by developing collective bargaining at the grassroots level, enterprise-level unions will be transformed into labour organizations that genuinely represent the rights and interests of workers and once again become a functioning part of the ACFTU. In short, a collective bargaining system can fundamentally protect workers' rights and provide the ACFTU with an excellent opportunity to rebuild itself as a genuinely representative trade union.

The Erosion of Collective Bargaining Threatens Human Rights in the United Kingdom and the World

Keith Ewing

Keith Ewing is professor of public law at King's College London and the author of Bonfire of the Liberties: New Labour, Human Rights, and the Rule of Law. *In the following viewpoint, he says that the governor of the state of Wisconsin is attempting to roll back collective bargaining rights. He adds that Britain, Greece, and the European Union are also trying to restrict workers' rights to bargain collectively. He says that this violates international standards and is an assault on basic human rights and dignity.*

As you read, consider the following questions:

1. What does Ewing say Martin Luther King was doing when he was assassinated in 1968?

2. What changes has the European Commission demanded of Greece, according to Ewing?

3. According to Ewing, trade unions and collective bargaining are important as a means of what?

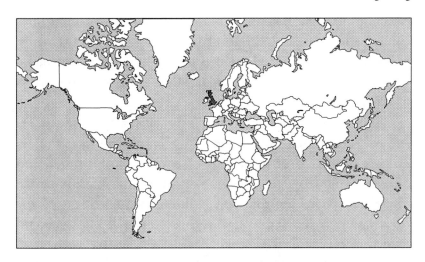

Dr Martin Luther King was assassinated in Memphis on this day [April 4] in 1968. He was there to support striking sanitation workers, fighting for the right to have their union recognised by their employer; fighting for the right to collective bargaining.

Solidarity

Today [April 4, 2011] is also a day of international solidarity with the public service workers of Wisconsin, whose right to bargain collectively has been stripped away by legislation sponsored by state governor Scott Walker, a man who has led the great state of Wisconsin to pariah status.

But as we stand in solidarity with brothers and sisters in Wisconsin, we do so in the knowledge that theirs is not a struggle confined to a single US state. Nor—as the neoliberal strategy of Governor Walker stretches to other states—is it a uniquely US problem. It is a global problem, demanding a global response.

European workers too are seeing the erosion of hard-won collective bargaining rights, also as a result of the greed of the bankers, who have emerged from the financial crisis unscathed. In the UK [United Kingdom] the erosion of bargaining rights is taking place by stealth. Although collective bargaining machinery still exists in local government for example, friends in public service unions tell me it is a long time since they had a collective agreement on pay or on other terms and conditions of employment.

Public sector unions are finding themselves on the sharp end of "section 188 notices", in which employers issue notices of mass dismissal (of thousands of employees at a time), and offer to re-employ the workers concerned on inferior terms. These new terms are imposed without the agreement of the trade union or the workers, who have no choice but to accept. Sometimes it involves a repudiation of a collective agreement, which the union is powerless to defend. Collective agreements in this country are not legally binding, and the only sanction open to workers and their unions—industrial action—is so fraught with legal dangers as to often be beyond use.

All this is being done under cover of an EU [European Union] directive that was designed to protect workers facing redundancy [layoff] by requiring the employer to give as much advance notice as possible and to consult with the union to find alternatives, to reduce numbers to be made redundant, and to ameliorate the consequences. Protective legislation is used as a licence by employers to undermine collective agreements and terms and conditions of employment.

European workers too are seeing the erosion of hard-won collective bargaining rights . . . as a result of the greed of the bankers, who have emerged from the financial crisis unscathed.

A Global Assault

But it is not only in the UK where the bankers are calling the shots. In Greece, workers and trade unions have been told by the European Commission that their labour laws are to be made more flexible, which means their collective agreements must become more decentralised, which means in turn that fewer people are to be protected by collective bargaining.

This marks a global assault on the human rights of workers everywhere. Claims about violations of human rights are not to be made lightly, for fear of devaluing a fragile currency. But workers' rights are human rights, and the right to bargain collectively is recognised by international law as an essential aspect of the right to freedom of association.

At international level the right to bargain collectively is expressly recognised by the two core conventions of the ILO [International Labour Organization], the UN [United Nations] agency of which 183 countries are members, all bound by a constitutional principle to promote freedom of association. Conventions fleshing out that principle impose duties on member states, which include a duty to promote collective bargaining.

This marks a global assault on the human rights of workers everywhere.

That principle is embedded not only in international standards, but in regional treaties as well, including the EU Charter of Fundamental Rights of 2000. But although there is now recognition at EU level of the right to bargain collectively, the European Commission is also promoting a "competitiveness pact" designed to reduce employment conditions and eliminate collective bargaining.

These attacks at EU level—undermining the post-80s Social Europe settlement—have attracted little publicity, though they have been strongly condemned. Even the traditionally mild-mannered and consensual ETUC [European Trade Union Confederation] has adopted an uncharacteristically strident position, condemning the EU "competitiveness pact" as an "attack on collective bargaining" leading Europe to a "dead end".

The Dignity of Labor

On the day before he died on 4 April 1968, Dr King addressed the sanitation workers of Memphis and famously said:

> "You are demanding that this city will respect the dignity of labour. So often we overlook the work and the significance of those who are not in professional jobs, of those who are not in the so-called big jobs. But let me say to you tonight that whenever you are engaged in work that serves humanity and is for the building of humanity, it has dignity and it has worth."

Dr King's vision of the dignity and worth of labour can only be realised by the very architecture that governments throughout the world now seem determined to destroy. In this country, our forebears saw clearly the importance of trade unions, and the role of collective bargaining as a means of raising wages, equalising incomes, stimulating demand, creating jobs and reducing unemployment.

As Dr King realised, the case for collective bargaining is not simply an economic one. It is about social justice.

But as Dr King realised, the case for collective bargaining is not simply an economic one. It is about social justice. It is about repudiating the idea that labour is a commodity, competing in a Darwinian "labour market". Above all, it is about ensuring that everyone is treated with equal respect, and paid a fair day's wage for a fair day's work.

In the United States, Collective Bargaining Harms Workers and Taxpayers

Robert Barro

Robert Barro is a professor of economics at Harvard University. In the following viewpoint, he argues that public employee unions restrict workers' right to work and also harm taxpayers. Additionally, he argues that public employees have gained excessive benefits. He says that benefits for public employee unions should be rolled back and that collective bargaining rights for such unions should be eliminated. He praises Wisconsin for taking steps in this direction and hopes that other states will follow suit.

As you read, consider the following questions:

1. When and how does Barro say labor unions obtained exemption from antitrust laws?
2. What evidence does Barro present to show that right-to-work states have superior economic growth?
3. What states does Barro think may move to limit collective bargaining rights for public employee unions?

How ironic that Wisconsin has become ground zero for the battle between taxpayers and public-employee labor unions. Wisconsin was the first state to allow collective bar-

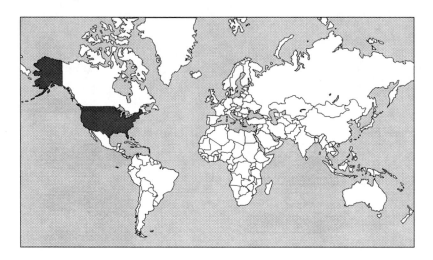

gaining for government workers (in 1959), following a tradition where it was the first to introduce a personal income tax (in 1911, before the introduction of the current form of individual income tax in 1913 by the federal government).

Not a Civil Liberty

Labor unions like to portray collective bargaining as a basic civil liberty, akin to the freedoms of speech, press, assembly and religion. For a teachers union, collective bargaining means that suppliers of teacher services to all public school systems in a state—or even across states—can collude with regard to acceptable wages, benefits and working conditions. An analogy for business would be for all providers of airline transportation to assemble to fix ticket prices, capacity and so on. From this perspective, collective bargaining on a broad scale is more similar to an antitrust violation than to a civil liberty.

In fact, labor unions were subject to U.S. antitrust laws in the Sherman Antitrust Act of 1890, which was first applied in 1894 to the American Railway Union. However, organized labor managed to obtain exemption from federal antitrust laws in subsequent legislation, notably the Clayton Antitrust Act of 1914 and the National Labor Relations Act of 1935.

Remarkably, labor unions are not only immune from antitrust laws but can also negotiate a "union shop," which requires nonunion employees to join the union or pay nearly equivalent dues. Somehow, despite many attempts, organized labor has lacked the political power to repeal the key portion of the 1947 Taft-Hartley Act that allowed states to pass right-to-work laws, which now prohibit the union shop in 22 states. From the standpoint of civil liberties, the individual right to work—without being forced to join a union or pay dues—has a much better claim than collective bargaining. (Not to mention that "right to work" has a much more pleasant, liberal sound than "collective bargaining.") The push for right-to-work laws, which haven't been enacted anywhere but Oklahoma over the last 20 years, seems about to take off.

From this perspective, collective bargaining on a broad scale is more similar to an antitrust violation than to a civil liberty.

The current pushback against labor-union power stems from the collision between overly generous benefits for public employees—notably for pensions and health care—and the fiscal crises of state and local governments. Teachers and other public-employee unions went too far in convincing weak or complicit state and local governments to agree to obligations, particularly defined-benefit pension plans, that created excessive burdens on taxpayers.

In recognition of this fiscal reality, even the unions and their Democratic allies in Wisconsin have agreed to Gov. Scott Walker's proposed cutbacks of benefits, as long as he drops the restrictions on collective bargaining. The problem is that this "compromise" leaves intact the structure of strong public-employee unions that helped to create the unsustainable fiscal situation; after all, the next governor may have less fiscal discipline. A long-run solution requires a change in structure, for example, by restricting collective bargaining for public employees and, to go further, by introducing a right-to-work law.

There is evidence that right-to-work laws—or, more broadly, the pro-business policies offered by right-to-work states—matter for economic growth. In research published in 2000, economist Thomas Holmes of the University of Minnesota compared counties close to the border between states with and without right-to-work laws (thereby holding constant an array of factors related to geography and climate). He found that the cumulative growth of employment in manufacturing (the traditional area of union strength prior to the rise of public-employee unions) in the right-to-work states was 26 percentage points greater than that in the non-right-to-work states.

The Next Battleground

Beyond Wisconsin, a key issue is which states are likely to be the next political battlegrounds on labor issues. In fact, one can interpret the extreme reactions by union demonstrators and absent Democratic legislators in Wisconsin not so much as attempts to influence that state—which may be a lost cause—but rather to deter politicians in other states from taking similar actions. This strategy may be working in Michigan, where Gov. Rick Snyder recently asserted that he would not "pick fights" with labor unions.

In general, the most likely arenas are states in which the governor and both houses of the state legislature are Republican (often because of the 2010 elections), and in which substantial rights for collective bargaining by public employees currently exist. This group includes Indiana, which has recently been as active as Wisconsin on labor issues; ironically, Indiana enacted a right-to-work law in 1957 but repealed it in 1965. Otherwise, my tentative list includes Michigan, Pennsylvania, Maine, Florida, Tennessee, Nebraska (with a nominally nonpartisan legislature), Kansas, Idaho, North Dakota and South Dakota.

Scott Walker, Governor of Wisconsin, on Reform and Unions

Beyond helping to balance current and future budgets, our reforms [in Wisconsin] will also make our government work better.

In 2010, Megan Sampson was named an Outstanding First Year Teacher in Wisconsin. A week later, she received a layoff notice from the Milwaukee Public Schools. So why would one of the best new teachers be one of the first let go? Because her collective bargaining contract requires staffing decisions to be made based on seniority.

Ms. Sampson received a layoff notice because the union leadership would not accept reasonable changes to their contract. Instead, they hid behind a collective bargaining agreement that costs the taxpayers more than $101,000 per year for each teacher; a contract which protects a 0% contribution for health insurance premiums; and a contract that forces schools to staff based on seniority and union rules.

Our budget reforms allow school districts to assign staff based on merit and performance. That keeps great teachers like Ms. Sampson in the classroom.

US House Committee on Oversight and Government Reform, Testimony of Governor Scott Walker (R-WI), April 14, 2011.

The national fiscal crisis and recession that began in 2008 had many ill effects, including the ongoing crises of pension and health care obligations in many states. But at least one positive consequence is that the required return to fiscal discipline has caused reexamination of the growth in economic and political power of public-employee unions. Hopefully, embattled politicians like Gov. Walker in Wisconsin will maintain their resolve and achieve a more sensible long-term structure for the taxpayers in their states.

South Africa Has Moved Toward Greater Centralization of Trade Unions

Johann Maree

Johann Maree is professor emeritus of sociology at the University of Cape Town. In the following viewpoint, he says that South Africa has moved toward greater centralization of unions. In part, he says, this is because of the end of a repressive apartheid government and greater freedom to unionize. He says that it is also because of the growth of black unions, which pushed hard for centralization. He notes that the trend toward centralization in South Africa is opposed to the trend in the rest of the world, which has been toward less unionization.

As you read, consider the following questions:

1. What is the classification of racial groups in South Africa, according to Maree?
2. What does Maree say forced the recognition of black trade unions in South Africa?
3. What labor trend in South Africa is the *same* as trends in the rest of the world, according to Maree?

Collective bargaining trends in South Africa have often moved in the opposite direction to global trends over the past thirty years. When collective bargaining decentralised in

Johann Maree, "Trends in Collective Bargaining: Why South Africa Differs from Global Trends," ILERA, www.ilera-online.org, pp. 1–4, 8–9. Reprinted by permission of the author.

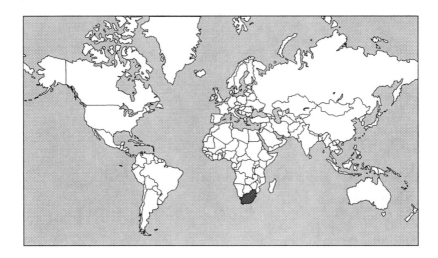

many countries it became more centralised in South Africa; when trade union density declined it increased in South Africa. One explanation has been the emergence of a less repressive regime in South Africa that enabled the pent-up demand for trade unions to be met. Although there is some validity in this perception it is incomplete and inadequate.

This [viewpoint] presents an alternative and more comprehensive explanation that situates collective bargaining in South Africa in its historical context. In doing so, it provides a political, economic and social analysis of collective bargaining trends in South Africa.

South Africa's Apartheid Heritage and Collective Bargaining

In order to understand the significance of the issues discussed in this [viewpoint] it is important to have a grasp of South Africa's demographics and population groups. The classification of the South African population is based on the country's history and consists of four groups: Blacks, Whites, Coloured people, and Asians. Blacks are indigenous Africans, Whites are descendants of European settlers, Asians come mainly from India but also from elsewhere in East Asia. Coloured people are the descendants of the aboriginal Khoi and San people, slaves from Southeast Asia, and the result of combined Black and White parentage.

As a result of the apartheid heritage there are still significant differences in the socioeconomic circumstances of the four population groups. Blacks are the poorest and make up the overwhelming majority (79.5 per cent) of the population of 47.5 million in 2006. Whites are the wealthiest and constitute slightly more than 9 per cent of the population. There are almost as many Coloured people as Whites in the country while the Asian population group is the smallest making up only 2.5 per cent of the population.

For the first 55 years of their existence the industrial councils statutorily denied Black workers, who have always constituted the overwhelming majority of the working class, access to centralised collective bargaining.

The centrepiece of collective bargaining legislation in South Africa was the Industrial Conciliation Act of 1924. It made provision for the establishment of industrial councils as the core centralised collective bargaining institution that still exists (except that the name was changed to bargaining council in 1995). For the first 55 years of their existence the industrial councils statutorily denied Black workers, who have always constituted the overwhelming majority of the working class, access to centralised collective bargaining. This was done by not allowing them to belong to or establish registered trade unions, the only unions that were allowed to join industrial councils.

However the emergence of democratic Black trade unions with strong workplace organisation in the early 1970s as well as increasing international pressure against the apartheid state forced the South African state in 1979 to allow Black trade unions to become registered and thus able to join industrial councils. This constituted a fundamental turning point for employment relations in South Africa. During the 1980s and early 1990s the industrial relations landscape changed dramatically as Black unions grew rapidly, gained recognition from employers, and started participating in industrial councils. These unions drastically shifted power relations in negotiations and brought a new dynamic to collective bargaining in South Africa.

Further transformation of collective bargaining took place after the political transformation of South Africa in 1994. Universal franchise brought Black majority rule to South Africa for the first time ever under the ruling African National Congress (ANC) with Nelson Mandela as the first president of the new South Africa. The new government rapidly passed a cluster of labour laws that entrenched worker and trade union rights very strongly. The centrepiece for collective bargaining was the Labour Relations Act of 1995 that extended full collective bargaining rights to almost the entire public service as well as domestic and farm workers and changed the name of industrial councils to bargaining councils. The act did not impose the duty to bargain was not imposed by the legislation, but the act did strengthen trade union organisational rights at the workplace.

The remainder of this [viewpoint] examines the changes in collective bargaining that have taken place in South Africa since 1979.

Collective Bargaining Trends in South Africa 1979–2008

Before 1979 industrial councils were the dominant collective bargaining institutions in South Africa. They could be established by registered trade unions and employer associations in a particular region and sector of the economy if the Minister of Labour deemed them to be sufficiently representative. Until 1979 Black workers were excluded from participating in the industrial council system. They were excluded from the definition of employees and could not belong to registered trade unions. As a result they did not have direct representation on the councils.

Industrial councils' principal functions were to negotiate and implement wages and working conditions for employees covered by the council. Once an agreement had been successfully negotiated the Minister of Labour would publish it in the Government Gazette whereupon the agreement had the force of law. If the parties to the council were deemed sufficiently representative by the minister the agreement could be extended to all employees in that particular sector and region. Provision was also made for exemption from the agreement upon appeal. It was usually small firms not party to the industrial councils that appealed against the extension of the agreement on the grounds that they could not afford the extra cost that the agreement incurred.

Before 1979 industrial councils were the dominant collective bargaining institutions in South Africa.

Just prior to 1978 there were 102 industrial councils in existence. Although the original intention of the legislators was that industrial councils should be national and hence that bargaining would be highly centralised, only 13 per cent of the councils were national in 1978. Over 50 per cent of the councils were regional, covering either the whole or part of one of the four provinces. Almost a third of the councils were local, usually operating within a city or town, while six had only a single employer.

At the end of the 1970s industrial councils were at their peak. From then there has been a decline in the number of councils. . . . During the first period (1978–92) there was a strong decline in national and regional councils with local councils remaining steady. But during the second period

(1992–2004) regional, local, and single company councils declined steeply while there was actually an increase in national councils. There are a number of reasons for these diverse trends.

The Effect of Black Unions

In 1979 Black trade unions were able to register for the first time. Their new legal status led to recognition by employers and the unions grew explosively during the 1980s. The signed up membership of the Black unions that started up during the early 1970s increased more than fourfold from 70,150 in 1979 to 299,552 in 1983 while the number of recognition agreements by companies shot up from a mere 5 in 1979 to 406 in 1983. At first the unions were hostile to industrial councils and opposed to joining them because they feared that they would be dominated by employers and White trade unions on the councils; but from 1982 onwards the Black unions started joining councils. Where the unions were strong nationally they started to thrive, but some unions' suspicions and hostilities lingered and they deliberately set about collapsing the councils once they had joined them. The unions were inadvertently assisted in this by some large employers who strongly adhered to free market principles and withdrew from the regulatory world of industrial councils.

In 1979 Black trade unions were able to register for the first time.

During the 1980s the South African government also strongly imbibed the free market ideology and was keen to reduce labour regulation. Consequently it tightened up the representivity requirements for bargaining councils and made the gazetting of agreements and their extensions more difficult. These measures also served to weaken industrial councils and contributed to the demise of the ones that were frail already.

During the second period (1992–2004) a new dynamic set in. Some of the Black trade unions had grown into large and powerful national unions. By 1996 total trade union membership including all unions (not only Black unions) had increased to just over three million with a union density of 57.5 per cent in the private nonagricultural sectors of the economy. In order to consolidate their power they wanted to bargain nationally with employers. Those unions that were on regional bargaining councils started lobbying for the merger of the councils into one national council. This happened in the case of the clothing industry when five regional clothing councils merged into one national council in May 2002. In addition, in industries where there were no bargaining councils, but strong Black trade unions, the unions started agitating for the establishment of a bargaining council. Thus, for instance, a National Bargaining Council for the Chemical Industry (BCCI) was established in December 2001. For the past few years the large and powerful National Union of Mineworkers (NUM) with 270,500 members has been agitating for the establishment of a national bargaining council in the mining industry, but thus far the Chamber of Mines has not agreed to it even though centralized collective bargaining between them has been taking place for decades.

In summary, bargaining councils have declined in number to less than half their 1979 total, but they underwent a structural change towards more centralised bargaining. This was principally due to the emergence of large national Black unions that came to appreciate the advantages of centralized national level bargaining. . . .

Collective Bargaining Trends Globally 1979–2008

The trend observed in collective bargaining and trade unionism in South Africa has by and large been opposite to global trends. Whereas collective bargaining became more centralised

Trade Unions in South Africa

South Africa's trade union movement, the largest and most disciplined on the continent, has played an influential role in determining labour market and industrial relations policies in the country. Its role in dismantling apartheid legislation and practices in the workplace remains one of its major achievements. During the apartheid era it succeeded in making employers appreciate the benefits of negotiating with employees through their representative unions.

SouthAfrica.info,
"Trade Unions in South Africa."
ww.southafrica.info.

and trade union density increased over the past quarter of a century in South Africa, the converse was happening in many other countries in the world.

In a study of industrial relations trends in nine countries, Australia, France, Germany, Italy, Japan, South Korea, Taiwan, United Kingdom and United States of America, [S.] Ouchi and [T.] Araki . . . observed that,

'in almost all countries mentioned above there are some common tendencies: labour unions are declining and labour density is decreasing; determination of working conditions at the enterprise level is gradually becoming widespread; pressure for disadvantageous modification of working conditions in return for employment security is growing; derogation and deregulation are being more widely needed and accepted.'

There has thus been a trend of falling union density and decentralisation of collective bargaining in most of the nine countries.

But South Africa has also experienced something in common with the rest of the world, namely the pursuit of increased flexibility in the regulation of labour by employers. As [G.] Standing has pointed out, this growing labour flexibility has been wide-ranging: It entailed wage and labour cost flexibility, employment (numerical) flexibility, and work process (functional) flexibility. He sees calls for flexibility as 'little more than ill-designed masks for proposals to lower wages or worker protection'.

The reasons why trends in collective bargaining and union density in South Africa have differed from those of many other countries in the world are thus not adequately explained by attributing them to the emergence of a less repressive regime in South Africa that enabled the pent-up demand for trade unions to be met.

The trend observed in collective bargaining and trade unionism in South Africa has by and large been opposite to global trends.

The core explanation lies in the emergence of a Black trade union movement in South Africa during the 1970s. It had to struggle for its survival in the first few years of its existence and, once that was achieved, for recognition from employers and the state. The crucial moment came in 1979 when the apartheid regime, partly forced by international pressure, reversed its policy and passed legislation that gave Black trade unions the same rights accorded to White trade unions. That was the turning point. Black trade unions grew rapidly in size and strength to become a significant economic and political force at national levels from the mid-1980s onwards. As large Black national unions established themselves, they joined bargaining councils. Where a national Black union joined a number of regional councils in the same industry, the unions pressurised employers' associations on these regional councils to agree to their amalgamation into a national bargaining council. In other industries, where there were no bargaining councils, large national Black trade unions successfully managed to lobby for the creation of a national bargaining council. Hence collective bargaining in South Africa became more centralised from the 1990s onwards. At the same time trade union density grew.

Another reason collective bargaining centralisation and trade union density increased during the 1990s was due to the extension of collective bargaining institutions into the public sector. Large national public sector bargaining councils were set up and the unionisation of almost all the public servants into large national unions took place. This increased union density considerably. Hence South Africa moved in the opposite direction to many countries as far as collective bargaining and trade unionism was concerned.

The core explanation [for greater centralization in South African unions] lies in the emergence of a Black trade union movement in South Africa during the 1970s.

On the other hand, South Africa moved in step with the rest of the world by increasing flexibility and reducing the regulation of labour. This was due to a combination of developments. Political transformation to a democracy in 1994 opened the South African economy to trade with the rest of the world after decades of sanctions and boycotts by the international community. This was coupled with trade liberalisation as tariffs were lowered and quotas lifted. In addition, production strategies switched to flexible specialization. Employers responded to these combined forces by introducing as much flexibility as they could into the employment relationship. Non-standard employment grew through the processes of casualisation, externalisation and informalisation.

South Africa experienced both opposing and similar trends in collective bargaining, trade unionism and labour regulation as many other countries in the world.

Canada May Move Toward Weakening Trade Unions

Tom Sandborn

Tom Sandborn is a contributing editor of the British Columbia online magazine the Tyee. *In the following viewpoint, he argues that America's anti-union climate has affected Canada. Canadian prime minister Stephen Harper and conservative forces in Canada, inspired by anti-union efforts in Wisconsin, are working to weaken public sector unions. Sandborn says unions are fighting back with rallies and initiatives targeted at the banks that helped encourage the Wisconsin assault on unions. Sandborn concludes that unions are threatened in Canada, but notes that unions are more popular and have more legal protections in Canada than they do in the United States.*

As you read, consider the following questions:

1. What do Palacios and Veldhuis say Canada should do to limit union power?

2. What is M&I's relationship with Scott Walker, and what is BMO's relationship with M&I, according to Sandborn?

3. Why does Griffin Cohen say that Canada is different from the United States in regard to unions?

Tom Sandborn, "Will America's Anti-Union Spasm Engulf Canada?," *The Tyee*, April 18, 2011. Reprinted by permission.

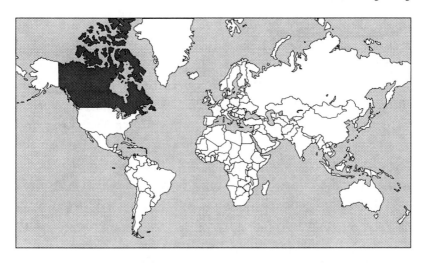

The right-wing drive to strip public sector unions of contracts, pensions and rights won over years of service and collective bargaining—it's not just a Wisconsin story anymore. All over the U.S., Republican politicians are making headway in trying to copy the sweeping rollback by Wisconsin's Tea Party–backed [the Tea Party is a loosely affiliated right-wing group that advocates for small government] governor, Scott Walker.

Following Scott Walker

And here in Canada, both the Right and the union movement are alert to the potential for a spillover effect.

"We Need Scott Walker Here" [that is, in Canada] was the headline topping an article by Fraser Institute economists Milagros Palacios and Niels Veldhuis published in the *Financial Post* three weeks before the current election got under way. At a moment when poll numbers indicated [Prime Minister Stephen] Harper's Conservatives were verging into majority territory [that is, a majority in Parliament], Palacios and Veldhuis wrote "our politicians should take a page from Governor Walker's playbook and roll back the wage premium. Canadian governments should also restrict collective bargaining in the public sector by banning the right to strike for public sector employees and having their wages and benefits linked to private sector counterparts."

The moment is hardly lost on British Columbia's trade unions, either. In recent weeks, their members and supporters have rallied for a demonstration in downtown Vancouver and a larger action at the Peace Arch border [a monument on the US/Canada border], voicing support for workers in Wisconsin and across the U.S. who they say are facing Tea Party–inspired assaults on collective bargaining rights. This was not just an exercise in international solidarity, speakers insisted at both actions. A real danger exists, they argued, that similar damage to workers' rights could happen in Canada.

A real danger exists . . . that similar damage to workers' rights could happen in Canada.

Bank of Montreal and Union Busters

The downtown Vancouver rally, held March 22 [2011] outside the annual general meeting of Bank of Montreal [BMO] shareholders at the posh Four Seasons Hotel, was prompted by the recent decision by BMO to buy an American bank, Marshall & Ilsley (M&I). M&I executives were key financial backers of Governor Walker, whose administration brought in the union-busting laws that provoked weeks of mass demonstrations in Wisconsin in February and March.

Critics have raised questions about why BMO bought an underperforming Midwestern bank, paid off its enormous Troubled Asset Relief Program debt to the U.S. government and then issued the M&I executives who had created that debt multi-million dollar severance payments.

More than 700 pieces of anti-union legislation similar to Wisconsin's new law are now being proposed in the U.S., with efforts to carve away union rights occurring in nearly every state, the *L.A. Times* reported.

"If BMO is OK with backing union busters in the U.S.," asked the fliers distributed outside the bank meeting, "what are their plans for Canada?"

Laurie Grant, a media spokesperson for Bank of Montreal, told the *Tyee* that BMO's Canadian experience would be helpful to the American bank they had acquired. She said her firm had no choice but to make the controversial severance payments to M&I executives. The payments were, she insisted, contractual and legal. She said that BMO had no intentions of taking anti-union positions in Canada, noting that no Canadian bank workers are unionized.

The economic crisis was not caused by good paycheques or decent pensions, but rather the declining number of these in both the private and the public sector.

"Non-union is the industry standard," she said.

On April 2, a rally co-sponsored by the B.C. Federation of Labour and union centrals from Washington State and Oregon drew more than 2,000 demonstrators to the Peace Arch border crossing. The event was one of more than 1,000 "We Are One" rallies held across the U.S., organized by the AFL-CIO [American Federation of Labor and Congress of Industrial Organizations], America's largest union umbrella group. . . .

According to B.C. Fed [British Columbia Federation of Labour] president Jim Sinclair, writing in an editorial published in the Victoria *Times Colonist* with Jeff Johnson and Tom Chamberlain, officers from the two American labour groups that co-sponsored the Peace Arch rally:

"The same right-wing leaders who advocated shipping good private sector jobs overseas are now claiming to represent the people against public sector wages and benefits. The economic crisis [of 2008] was not caused by good paycheques or decent pensions, but rather the declining num-

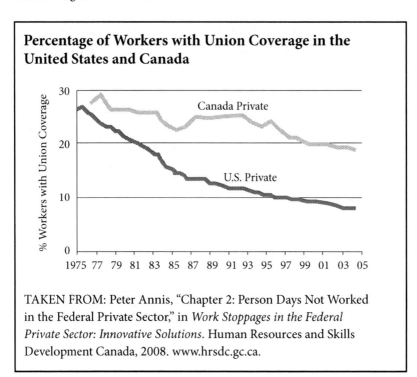

Percentage of Workers with Union Coverage in the United States and Canada

TAKEN FROM: Peter Annis, "Chapter 2: Person Days Not Worked in the Federal Private Sector," in *Work Stoppages in the Federal Private Sector: Innovative Solutions*. Human Resources and Skills Development Canada, 2008. www.hrsdc.gc.ca.

ber of these in both the private and the public sector.... With unions gone, the wealthy will simply get more and more of what they want."

What the rich want in America, and may well set out to achieve in Canada as well, is a far weaker union movement than has existed on this continent in many decades, according to teachers' union officer Betsy Kippers, who attended the BMO stockholder' meeting armed with proxies for 3,225 shares in the Canadian bank. Kippers, a teacher with more than 30 years of experience and now vice president of the 98,000 member Wisconsin Education [Association] Council, spoke with the *Tyee* the day before her appearance at the bank's AGM [annual general meeting].

"What the governor is doing in Wisconsin," Kippers said, "was never about fiscal needs. This is all about taking back rights from working class families."

"Move Your Money" Campaign

Marc Norberg, a burly officer from the Sheet Metal Workers International Association who attended the BMO meeting with Kippers, told the *Tyee* about a fight-back campaign his organization has helped to develop in the U.S. Urging union members and pension funds to withdraw their money from M&I branches, the "Move Your Money" campaign has been conducting demonstrations outside 60 to 70 M&I branches every week, and in two cases prompted large enough withdrawals that the affected branches had to shut down for the day.

"What's wild about this effort," Norberg said, "is that often customers go into the bank, withdraw all their money and come out and show the withdrawal slips to our demonstrators."

Norberg said that local businesses had been dropping by his group's picket lines with coffee and snacks to support their campaign.

Not everyone, of course, supports union efforts. Kippers said that the attack across America on trade union rights is being orchestrated by the newly emerged and powerful right-wing Tea Party–type groups.

"It's all about privatization and corporate wealth," she charged. "We have to move now from being a protest to being a movement. Governor Walker has awakened a sleeping giant."

There was little sign of sleepiness at the Canada-U.S. border crossing at the Peace Arch on April 2, as a boisterous crowd of more than 2,000 cheered speakers from both sides of the border issuing calls for solidarity and shared fight back.

"I look at Stephen Harper and I think, 'There's our Wisconsin. He hates unions. He always has,'" Sinclair told the crowd.

B.C. Teachers' Federation president Susan Lambert, who acted as rally MC, took a moment to send a Twitter message from the stage, "Democracy. You use it or you lose it."

Canadian Labour Congress head Ken Georgetti told the crowd he had never seen such concern and support from Canadians as he was seeing in response to the attacks on Wisconsin workers.

"I was in Washington, D.C., and I told the leadership of the AFL-CIO that we'll be there in support," Georgetti said.

While we should be concerned, we should also recognize that the situation in Canada is different.

He closed his speech by noting that nothing in either of Canada's official languages was sufficiently strong to express his response to Governor Walker and his anti-union accomplices. However, citing his own Italian heritage, Georgetti said he had one message for the governor, a message he illustrated with a classic Italian gesture involving using one hand to slap his bicep while brandishing the other in a clenched fist. Voices from the crowd provided the verbal version—"Va Fongool!" (an Americanized pronunciation of the Italian curse *vaffanculo* or *vai in culo*.)

Marjorie Griffin Cohen, who teaches economics and women's studies at SFU [Simon Fraser University], has been watching the attempts in the U.S. to reduce the power of public sector unions with interest.

"When you attack public sector unions, you are attacking women," Griffin Cohen told the *Tyee*. "Can what's happening in the U.S. happen in Canada? Of course it can, and in fact it has happened. Just look at the BC Liberals' assaults on health care workers' and teachers' rights, both since overturned by the courts. While we should be concerned, we should also recognize that the situation in Canada is different."

In Canada, she said, unions are still stronger than in the U.S., and have been able to win recognition that collective bargaining is a Charter-protected right [referring to the Canadian Charter of Rights and Freedoms, which is part of the Constitution of Canada].

French Unions Threaten Workers' Well-Being

Spencer Fernando

Spencer Fernando is the international comment coordinator for the Manitoban, *the student newspaper for the University of Manitoba in Canada. In the following viewpoint, he argues that changing demographics require a change in pensions and a later retirement age. He argues that French unions striking against an increase in the retirement age are unrealistic and that they hurt society. He concludes that unions have outlived their usefulness and that they now care only about their leadership rather than about the well-being of their members.*

As you read, consider the following questions:

1. According to Fernando, how have demographics in Canada changed between 2001 and 2006?
2. What unions does Fernando say do not act against the interests of the people?
3. Why does Fernando believe we should make sure that we sustain the baby boomers' standard of living?

As the world recovers from the global financial crises, governments are beginning to realize that there is a deeper flaw in our systems of social services. As the average age of the population in many Western countries increases, due both to

Spencer Fernando, "A Refusal to Face Reality," *The Manitoban*, September 28, 2010. Reprinted by permission.

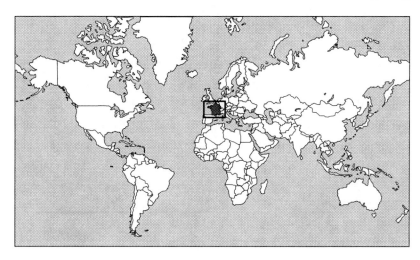

medical advancements and low birth rates, the proportion of workers to those receiving benefits is changing. As our parents' generation—the baby boomers—move into retirement, the burden will fall to us to pay for their continued standard of living. Here at home [in Canada], the retirement age is 65, and between 2001 and 2006 the number of Canadians between the ages of 55–64 increased 28 per cent.

Ballooning Costs

France is facing this problem acutely, as they struggle to get their budget deficit under control, and manage the ballooning costs of their social welfare programs. French President Nicolas Sarkozy has proposed raising the retirement age from 60 to 62 years old. This relatively minor change, one that is in my opinion necessary to secure the overall future of the French economy, has met with massive protests organized by unions. In my view, this is a short-sighted and selfish effort by unions to protect the narrow interests of their own leadership, as opposed to serving the common good of their own members and of the French people.

It is important to be clear that not all unions are acting against the interests of the people. Many unions for police, firefighters, nurses, etc., do a great job of looking out for the interests of both their members and society as a whole. But in my view, what we see in France, with unions crippling the transportation system and further damaging the economy, shows that they have become out of touch with the average worker and their families. It seems that in the face of threatening economic realities, unions have time and time again reverted back to tired and failed solutions, which involve either raising taxes on hardworking people to pay for bloated and excessive union dues, or raising taxes on the "rich," who more often than not are actually small business owners who are the backbone of most Western economies.

What I see in the actions of the French unions and in their efforts to create civil unrest and disruption is a complete refusal to face economic reality, and a failure to heed their own creed of sacrifice. The attitude exhibited by the unions in France, and many other Western countries, is an attitude of wanting to take but never to give. They want others to sacrifice, but they don't want to sacrifice anything themselves.

In the face of threatening economic realities, unions have time and time again reverted back to tired and failed solutions.

Unions Have Outlived Their Usefulness

Unions once served an essential purpose. Throughout the industrial revolution workers were often treated no better than slaves. It was essential for workers to fight for their basic human rights, and unions brought necessary changes. Today, though, with a few rare exceptions, unions no longer fight for progress, they fight against it. They no longer fight for the rights of their members; they fight to control them. Whereas it was once unions who wanted workers to have freedom and choice, it is now small businesses that promote the true interests of workers. The unions see their power weakening, and they are afraid. So as we see in France, they are lashing out in anger.

The economic problems of the world will not be solved through anger or from imposing systems of control upon people. As many Eastern economies rise, the West will have to adapt. We will succeed only if we are rational and realistic about the economic challenges we face.

We owe it to previous generations to make sure that we sustain their standard of living in their retirement years. They built a world of unprecedented prosperity for us, and the least we can do is honor their effort and hard work by providing for them. But to achieve this, we cannot allow narrow-minded union groups to put the interests of their leaders above their own members and every individual. The foolish attitude of thinking you can consume more money without producing more value will hit a dead end called bankruptcy. As Western economies take steps to avoid this fate, unions are often standing in the way.

French Unions Protect Workers from Government

Aurelien Mondon

Aurelien Mondon is a political scientist, a writer, and the co-founder of the Melbourne Free University. In the following viewpoint, he argues that the French people are sick of the government of President Nicolas Sarkozy and of the way Sarkozy has favored the wealthy. Mondon says that workers are united against the raising of the retirement age. He notes that the strikes will probably not be as violent as those of May 1968, but he hopes they will result in a change in French politics.

As you read, consider the following questions:

1. What did Sarkozy promise the French people he would do for a few weeks if he were elected, according to Mondon?

2. What groups does Mondon say Sarkozy blamed to divert the attention of the French?

3. According to Mondon, how will the French government appeal to the authoritarian part of the French population?

The massive strikes in France [in 2010] mark the failure of the [French president Nicolas] Sarkozy government. Weeks of unrest, culminating in mass opposition to the raising of the

Aurelien Mondon, "French Protests a Rejection of Sarkozy's Politics of Blame," *Sydney Morning Herald*, October 25, 2010. Reprinted by permission of the author.

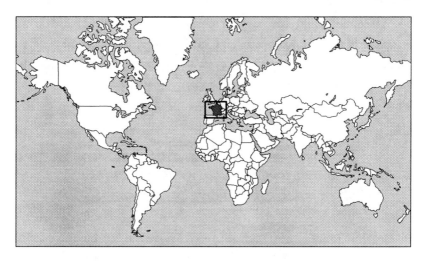

pension age, show a public deeply unhappy with their government and the direction it has taken the country.

Sarkozy and the Wealthy

Three years ago, a few days before the presidential elections that catapulted Nicolas Sarkozy into the presidency, the hyperactive candidate promised the French he would break away from the legacy of the student uprising of May 1968.

He promised that France would again stand tall, that he would put the French back into jobs and revive the morals and values whose lack had caused a deep "identity crisis".

With an unabashed populist rhetoric, neo-liberal Sarkozy even promised to put an end to savage capitalism, the appearance of which he blamed on the students' and workers' revolt.

While most of those who demonstrated in 1968 had done so for a fairer, more socialistic world, Sarkozy convinced the very people who had taken part in the events that it was their behaviour that had led to the excesses of capitalism; that the massive golden parachutes bosses received, despite poor performances, were the result of the emancipatory struggle that was May '68.

To emphasise his rupture with the old order, Sarkozy promised that if he were elected he would retire for a few weeks to a monastery to take a deeper sense of his function, before devoting himself to the task ahead. Sarkozy declared that he was now a friend of the people, not the rich, and that he understood their insecurities and fears for the future.

Sarkozy's most prominent economic reforms helped the wealthy, who received important tax deductions.

For Sarkozy's supporters, the wake-up call came soon after the second round of the elections. Early the next morning, the French learnt that their president had spent the night celebrating with his celebrity friends in one of the most exclusive nightclubs on the Champs-Elysées.

Sarkozy then retired briefly before taking office, but not to a monastery. Instead, he spent time on the yacht of French billionaire businessman and media magnate Vincent Bolloré.

Sarkozy's most prominent economic reforms helped the wealthy, who received important tax deductions. The lower classes were offered an increasingly repressive society and an ever-increasing number of scapegoats to blame for their feeling of social insecurity.

While, in Sarkozy's rhetoric, May '68 was the overarching reason for France's demise, many groups could, and indeed would, be blamed to divert the attention of the French.

Invoking populist right-wing rhetoric, he attacked suburban youth as "scum". Under a veil of pseudo-feminism, he attacked Muslims for being sexist and forcing their wives and sisters to wear the hijab [the head covering worn by Muslim women] (thus relegating the widespread issue of violence against women to the suburbs). And most recently, as his popularity slumped, Sarkozy expelled Roma people from France.

A French Postman Explains Why He Objects to Pension Reform

Frédéric Delouche, 40, postman: "My work is very hard on a physical level. I've been doing it for 10 years now and after a while various parts of your body begin to hurt—your back, your wrists, your joints. For people like me in arduous jobs, what this reform is suggesting is just not doable. I certainly can't see myself still coping with it at the age of 67.

Lizzy Davies,
"Nicolas Sarkozy Calls for Calm
as French Pension Protests Gather Pace,"
Guardian, October 19, 2010.

A New May 1968

Yet, this time, it seems Sarkozy's attacks on minorities were not enough to divert his people's attention from pension reforms. Discontent has been extreme in the past few weeks, and it was reported that up to 3.5 million people took to the streets on the sixth day of national demonstrations, leading some left-wing politicians to predict a "new May '68". While it is most unlikely France will again experience that intense social upheaval, a time when up to two-thirds of its population was on strike, the French are clearly discontented with their government and the politics it has played since its election. More than just a fight against tough pension reforms, French people of all ages and all classes seem to be expressing a desire for a different kind of politics, that of hope as opposed to the politics of fear and favouritism, which have climaxed since Sarkozy's election.

What the next step will be is uncertain. May '68 lost the population's support when demonstrators turned, or were turned, into rioters. It is clear that the government has learnt from such events. In 2005, when the French suburbs were set ablaze by excluded youth craving recognition and equal rights, the events were portrayed as little more than the senseless actions of gangs of rioters. Similarly, in 2010, the deeply troubling revolt of secondary school students has been portrayed in the French news as "guerilla warfare".

The French are clearly discontented with their government and the politics it has played since its election.

Images are swiftly employed and interpreted in such a way that will certainly appeal to the more authoritarian part of the French population, and to its desire for repression.

Without a doubt, more than the thirst for liberty and equality, it is the concept of fraternity between the many facets of the French population (age, religion and ethnic background) that will decide what comes next.

Now that the Senate has voted the pension reforms into law, only the unity of the French people could lead to their withdrawal and, possibly to French politics taking a turn for the better.

Periodical and Internet Sources Bibliography

The following articles have been selected to supplement the diverse views presented in this chapter.

Cecile Dehesdin	"High-School Unions and X-Rated Protest Signs: Why Do the French Strike So Much?," *Slate*, October 21, 2010. http://www.slate.com.
Robyn Dixon and Kylé Pienaar	"South Africa Unions Unhappy with Government's Wage Offer," *Los Angeles Times*, September 2, 2010.
Economist	"Unions in China: Strike Breakers," June 3, 2010.
Andrew England	"Walmart Takes on South Africa's Unions," *beyondbrics* (blog), January 17, 2011. http://blogs.ft.com.
Peter Ford	"Unions in China Still Feeble, but Gaining Foothold," *Christian Science Monitor*, September 29, 2008.
Sunny Lee	"Subjects for Collective Bargaining," *Korean Labor Law for Foreign Employers* (blog), December 31, 2008. www.koreanlaborlaw.com.
Ed Morrissey	"Chile Votes Down PEU Collective Bargaining," Hot Air, April 19, 2011. http://hotair.com.
Deroy Murdock	"The Right to Choose," *National Review Online*, March 11, 2011. www.nationalreview.com.
Meir Russ	"The Hollowing-Out of Wisconsin," *Guardian*, March 1, 2011.
Henry Samuel	"French Strikes: 3.5 Million Take to Streets to Protest Pension Reform," *Telegraph*, October 12, 2010.

GLOBALVIEWPOINTS

CHAPTER 3

Workplace Discrimination

Workplace Discrimination Is a Growing Problem in Asia

International Labour Organization (ILO)

The International Labour Organization (ILO) is the agency of the United Nations that deals with issues pertaining to international labor standards. In the following viewpoint, the ILO writes that workers in Asia continue to face traditional forms of discrimination, such as discrimination against women and migrants. The ILO says that new forms of discrimination—against the young, against the old, against those with disabilities, and against those with HIV/AIDS—are also increasing because of economic change and greater movements of people. The ILO notes that many countries in the region are, however, taking steps against discrimination.

As you read, consider the following questions:

1. What are LSOM jobs, and why does the ILO say that participation rates for women in such jobs are important?

2. What caste-based discrimination is faced by Dalits, according to the ILO?

3. What evidence does the ILO provide that persons with disabilities have much to contribute to the workplace?

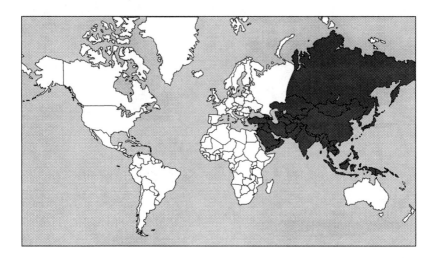

The Asia and Pacific region continues to experience traditional forms of discrimination, such as those based on gender and ethnic origin and is increasingly confronted with new forms of discrimination brought about by structural economic reforms, economic openness and greater movement of people.

Dynamic economic growth in Asia and the Pacific—driven by competitive integration into global markets for goods, services and investment—has spurred nearly 3 million Asian workers every year to seek employment abroad. These migrant workers face a variety of forms of discrimination in Europe and the Middle East, and increasingly within the Asian region itself.

A recent survey in Asia showed that one in six respondents who were living with HIV/AIDS had been discriminated in the workplace. A higher proportion of respondents experienced workplace discrimination in the Philippines (21 per cent) than in other countries in the region (15 per cent in Indonesia, 12 per cent in India and 7 per cent in Thailand).

Persistent Forms of Discrimination

Women still remain the largest group facing discrimination in terms of employment opportunities and wage gaps. An increase in employment rates for women over the past decade has not been even throughout the region. For example, in East Asia and the Pacific the female share of nonagricultural paid employment increased to 43.5 per cent whereas in South Asia the rate remains the world's lowest at only 16.5 per cent. Furthermore, two-thirds of all employed women in South Asia are working without pay.

An important measure of good-quality jobs available to women is their share of legislative, senior official or managerial (LSOM) jobs. Higher participation rates for women in LSOM jobs indicate a reduction of discriminatory barriers. Overall, the Asia and Pacific region experienced a rise of nearly 4 per cent in women in such positions over the past decade. However, South Asia shows only 8.6 per cent of women attaining these levels as compared to 24.8 per cent for East Asia and the Pacific.

Women still remain the largest group facing discrimination in terms of employment opportunities and wage gaps.

A persistent form of discrimination in South Asia has been caste-based [referring to the system in India that regulates jobs and marriages on the basis of hereditary groupings] discrimination. For example, this form confines Dalits to occupations often involving the most menial tasks such as "manual scavenging" or the removal of dead animals. Dalits are generally not accepted for any work involving contact with water or food for non-Dalits or entering a non-Dalit residence. They are thus excluded from a wide range of work opportunities in the area of production, processing or sale of food items, domestic work and the provision of certain services in the private and public sectors (e.g., office helpers).

Limited access to education, training and resources, such as land or credit, further impair their equal opportunities for access to non-caste-based occupations and decent work. The deprivation stemming from discrimination in all areas of their life leads to higher levels of poverty among Dalits compared to non-Dalits.

The growing numbers of migrant workers in the region face new forms of discrimination.

Equally serious and pervasive is discrimination confronting indigenous peoples in the region as in other regions as well. These peoples account for over 15 per cent of the world's poor, although they make up 5 per cent of the world's population. In Nepal, the indigenous peoples from the hill areas, the Hill Janajatis, lacking opportunities at home, make up [the] largest share of migrants working abroad (29 per cent) in countries other than India, and have the highest average remittance income (almost 35 per cent of annual household income).

Growing Discrimination Against Migrants

The growing numbers of migrant workers in the region face new forms of discrimination. Racial discrimination, xenophobia, intolerance are all reflected in low wages, long and exhausting working hours and violence.

In Japan, the United Nations special rapporteur on contemporary forms of racism, racial discrimination, xenophobia and related intolerance in a 2006 report expressed concern about discrimination against descendants of former Japanese colonies. Trade unions have taken important steps to address this: For example, Rengo [Japanese Trade Union Confederation], the largest union in Japan, has created a union for Chinese workers.

In Malaysia, the Malaysian Trades Union Congress (MTUC) have put in place mechanisms to ensure better protection of the 1.5 million documented migrant workers living in the country.

In Pakistan, official statistics show a growth since 2004 in the numbers of workers migrating from the tribal areas in search of jobs, mainly in the construction sector in the Gulf countries. Because of their limited access to official channels of migration and official travel documents, indigenous and tribal people appear to be more likely than other groups to become undocumented migrant workers. Indigenous women are especially vulnerable to falling prey to trafficking.

In China, the situation is slightly different where a swell of rural migrants—an estimated 150 million—are labouring in the coastal cities but are finding it difficult to obtain permits largely due to the constraints of the hukou system [which requires individuals to register as residents of a particular area]. Owing to their social status, rural migrants suffer from institutionalized discrimination. In some cities, authorities deny them access to better jobs so they end up working in informal, low-paid, menial jobs that urban workers refuse. Since rural migrants currently represent 40 per cent of the urban workforce this will remain an important social and economic concern for China.

In the past few years, the Chinese government has taken important steps to help disadvantaged rural migrant workers ... such as ensuring a guaranteed minimum wage, the enforcement of a labour contract system, as well as access to employment services and job training.

Newly Emerging Forms

New forms of discrimination are emerging in the region such as unfair treatment of both young and older persons, people with disabilities, those living with HIV/AIDS, and on the basis of sexual orientation. An additional challenge is the emergence of practices that penalize those with a genetic predisposition to developing certain diseases or those who have lifestyles considered unhealthy.

Disability Antidiscrimination Legislation in the Philippines

The Philippines Magna Carta for [Disabled Persons] is an explicit rights-based statute which contains guarantees of rights in a range of areas of life, including employment, education, health, social security, accessibility in the built environment and in relation to transport, political rights and the right to assemble and organize. Some of the provisions are expressed as guarantees of rights or in terms of the state's obligation to recognize particular rights; there are also provisions which are programmatic—for example, setting out incentives for employers who employ persons with disabilities, obliging the state to adopt appropriate rehabilitation and vocational training measures, and requiring the state to provide assistance for students with disabilities and establish special schools, and obliging state universities to conduct research on disability issues—as well as other measures, for example in relation to tax incentives for certain expenditures. Amendments to the act in 2007 included provisions mandating discounts on a range of goods and services for persons with disabilities, and protection against ridicule or vilification on the ground of disability. The act also provides for the secretary of justice to investigate alleged violations of the act and to commence legal action in certain cases.

Andrew Byrnes,
"Disability Discrimination Law and the Asian and Pacific Region,"
United Nations Economic and Social Committee for Asia
and the Pacific, January 21, 2011. www.unescap.org.

With some 470 million people with disabilities of working age, disability has become a major workplace issue. Although considerable variations exist across countries, persons with disabilities have activity rates well below the average of other working groups. This reflects, among other factors, their lower educational and skills development attainments, which, in turn, result from societal and institutional barriers to equal opportunities for people with disabilities in education and vocational training.

However, persons with disabilities have much to contribute to the workplace. Sixty-five per cent of Australian employers rated the financial cost of workplace accommodations as neutral and 20 per cent indicated an overall financial benefit. The average recruitment cost of an employee with a disability was only 13 per cent more than the average recruitment cost of an employee without a disability.

New forms of discrimination are emerging in the region such as unfair treatment of both young and older persons, people with disabilities, those living with HIV/ AIDS, and on the basis of sexual orientation.

DuPont has conducted surveys in a number of countries showing that over 35 years disabled employees perform equally or better compared to their colleagues without disabilities. Only 4 per cent of disabled people of working age require additional adjustments in the workplace. Costs are generally negligible. Marks & Spencer has shown that two-thirds of the adjustments for disabled people do not involve any costs.

The impact of HIV/AIDS on the workplace has become an important social and economic issue. Around 40 million people worldwide are living with HIV/AIDS. The epidemic is spreading rapidly also in Asia and central Asia with prevalence rising fastest among young adults (aged 15–29 years), especially girls and young women.

Stigma and discrimination on account of actual or perceived HIV/AIDS status are multiple and complex; they are hard to measure, and the data difficult to interpret. Stigma generally affects more women than men, even when they acquire the disease through their husbands. In an ILO [International Labour Organization] study in India, a survey conducted among 292 persons—42 per cent female with an average age of 30 years—showed that 90 per cent of women had been infected by their husbands. More women had suffered discrimination (74 per cent) than men (68 per cent).

Rapid developments in genetics and related new technologies have important implications for the workplace. Employers decide to exclude or dismiss employees whose genetic status shows a predisposition to developing a certain disease in the future. Making an employment decision on the basis of the probability of an individual's developing a certain disease, rather than on their actual capacity to perform their job, constitutes discrimination.

Trade unions are active in this field. The Australian Council of Trade Unions (ACTU) stated in 2002 that employers should not be allowed to gather genetic information about any employee. While criticizing employers for inappropriate collection of employees' genetic data, the Australian Law Reform Commission and Australian Health Ethics Commission declared that they would consider permitting the use of genetic testing, where reasonable and relevant, and in a way that balanced the interests of employers, employees and the public at large.

National and Regional Action

There have been encouraging developments in combating discrimination in the workplace. The governments of the Philippines and Japan have recently enacted laws that address sexual harassment as a form of discrimination. The law provides that both women and men shall be protected from sexual harassment, and requires employers to take workplace measures to address it.

In India, mobile crèches on construction sites have been created to cater for the children of migrant construction workers. At present the system of mobile crèches operates through a network of 450 day care centres, located on building sites and slum clusters in New Delhi, Mumbai and Pune and reaching out to 600,000 children.

There have been encouraging developments in combating discrimination in the workplace.

In New Zealand, the Equal Employment Opportunities (EEO) Trust, a joint initiative launched in 1992 by leading private and public sector employers to promote awareness of the business benefits of equal opportunities at the workplace, has developed jointly with the Recruitment and Consulting Services Association a publication targeting recruitment agencies and aimed at removing discriminatory practices.

In Sri Lanka, the concern over promoting equal opportunities at the workplace is reflected in the production of Guidelines for Company Policy on Gender Equity/Equality developed by the Employers' Federation of Ceylon (EFC) in cooperation with the ILO in 2006.

In Singapore, the Tripartite Declaration on Equal Remuneration for Men and Women Performing Work of Equal Value affirms the commitment of the government and the social partners to the principle embodied in Convention No. 100 [of the ILO, which states that men and women should receive equal pay]. The tripartite partners also agreed to insert an appropriate clause in collective agreements to ensure that employers adhere to the principle of equal remuneration for work of equal value.

Caste Discrimination in South Asian Communities in the United Kingdom Is a Serious Problem

Roger Green, Stephen Whittle, and Anti Caste Discrimination Alliance (ACDA)

Anti Caste Discrimination Alliance (ACDA) is an independent organization dedicated to eliminating caste discrimination in the United Kingdom and abroad; Roger Green is the director of the Centre for Community Research at the University of Hertfordshire; Stephen Whittle is a law professor at the University of Manchester. In the following viewpoint, the authors argue that caste discrimination is a serious problem within the Indian community in the United Kingdom. They say that Britain must do more to track and prevent this kind of discrimination.

As you read, consider the following questions:

1. According to this viewpoint, what do the Hindu Council UK and the Hindu Forum of Britain argue about caste discrimination in the United Kingdom?

2. What percentage of survey respondents do the authors say experienced caste discrimination, and what kind of discrimination did they suffer?

Roger Green, Stephen Whittle, and Anti Caste Discrimination Alliance (ACDA), "Executive Summary," *Hidden Apartheid—Voice of the Community: Caste and Caste Discrimination in the UK: A Scoping Study*, Anti Caste Discrimination Alliance, 2009, pp. 1–4. Reprinted by permission.

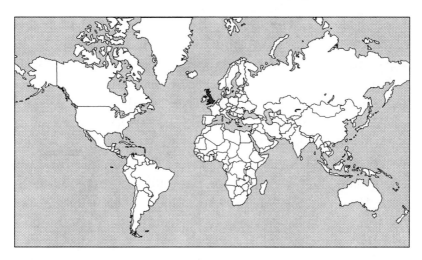

3. What do the authors recommend the government do to address caste discrimination in education?

This [viewpoint] sets out the results of a scoping study [that is, a study of the range or breadth of a phenomenon] conducted between August and October 2009 to establish how people know that the caste system [an Indian social system that prevents some people from holding certain jobs or from social contacts based on heredity] exists in the United Kingdom (UK) and, for those who had experienced caste discrimination, the setting it had occurred in and the impact it had had on them. Over 300 people participated in an online questionnaire and nine focus groups in England.

The Caste System Exists in the UK

Over the last 60 years, there has been a gradual increase in the numbers of people in the UK from the Indian subcontinent. These communities have settled here and brought with them their own social habits, norms and religious customs including the caste system.

The Hindu Council UK and the Hindu Forum of Britain have both acknowledged in their reports that the caste system exists in the UK. However, both bodies argue that caste discrimination is not endemic in the UK, and only plays a role in social interactions and personal choices like marriages, conversations and friendships. A number of academics and UK organisations, including the Anti Caste Discrimination Alliance (ACDA), Dalit Solidarity Network UK (DSN), Federation of Ambedkarite and Buddhist Organisations (FABO) and CasteWatchUK (CWUK), argue otherwise. They say that the caste system and the discrimination associated with it impacts in some form or other on the two million or so people in the UK from the Asian diaspora and extends beyond social interaction.

On 8 October 2009, Navi Pillay, the United Nations High Commissioner for Human Rights publicly condemned caste discrimination which affects 270 million people worldwide. Although other countries have laws to protect against caste discrimination—for example, the Constitution of India 1950 abolishes the practice of Untouchability [in which particular castes are ostracized] and makes caste discrimination unlawful—no such protection exists in the UK.

Although other countries have laws to protect against caste discrimination ... no such protection exists in the UK.

Key Findings

A preliminary search of the academic literature shows that this is an under-researched area. Both the online questionnaire and the focus groups confirm that the caste system exists in the UK and the associated lack of caste mobility is not consistent with the government's position of encouraging a more cohesive society.

A majority of the research participants identified negative experiences of the caste system and caste discrimination. For some, this had a traumatising effect on them resulting in low morale, low self-esteem, depression and anxiety.

71 percent of survey responses identified themselves as belonging to the so-called 'Dalit' community [a caste often discriminated against], 58 percent of survey responses confirmed they had been discriminated against because of their caste. 37 percent stated that this had occurred on several occasions. There are an estimated 175,000 Ravidassia [a religion followed by many Dalits] people in the UK. Based on the survey data, over 100,000 of this population alone may be victims of caste discrimination in the UK.

The majority—79 percent—of survey respondents stated they believed they would not be understood appropriately by the UK police service if they reported a 'hate crime' incident based on caste discrimination.

85 percent believed there was no legislation in place to protect them as victims of caste discrimination.

The government's decision to not include a clause in the Equality Bill 2009 to protect citizens against caste discrimination in the UK seems mainly to have been informed by the Hindu Forum of Britain and the Hindu Council UK's reports and representations—and an unrepresentative and restricted sample of 19 replies.

Employment

45 percent of people who responded to the survey stated that they had been either treated in a negative way by their co-workers (20 percent) or had comments made about them on account of their caste status (25 percent). 25 percent indicated that they had been informally excluded from social events, informal networks in the organisation or the 'grapevine' because of their caste. Similarly, nine percent stated that they believed they had missed promotion at work due to their caste, with a further ten percent stating that they had been underpaid because of their caste. Nine percent stated they had experienced

verbal abuse. Five percent had been subjected to threatening behaviour because of their caste.

Similar experiences came to light in the focus groups. For example, there was a case of a woman who believed she had been demoted from a good position at a local radio station when her line manager discovered her caste. Another workplace example was that of a manager of [a] bus company in Southampton who had to re-organise the shift system so that a "higher caste" inspector would not need to work with a "lower caste" bus driver.

There are increasing numbers of Indian companies setting up in Britain. Such companies may inadvertently import caste-based practices to the UK.

There was a case of a woman who believed she had been demoted from a good position at a local radio station when her line manager discovered her caste.

Recommendations:

1. Government to provide legal protection against caste discrimination for victims (or possible victims)

2. The DWP [Department for Work and Pensions], CBI [Confederation of British Industry], and the TUC [Trades Union Congress] to ensure that companies operating in Britain do not inadvertently import caste-based practices, and put monitoring in place to support all workers' and members' rights.

Education

Seven percent in the survey said that when they were under 12 years old they had been subjected to threatening behaviour and 16 percent to verbal abuse because of their caste.

10 percent of the perpetrators of caste discrimination for the under 12s were said to have been teachers, and 42 percent

fellow pupils. These survey results were supported by the numerous examples that came to light in the focus groups including caste-related bullying.

Recommendation:

Department for education and schools to provide guidance to statutory and voluntary organisations and local education authorities (LEAs) for teachers in schools to improve their understanding and skills in recognizing caste-based bullying and discrimination.

Provision of Goods and Services

Although the survey focused on the areas of provision of health care and social care services, other aspects of service provision including access to goods and facilities in places of worship (which often double as community centres) were highlighted during the focus groups.

Of the 43 out of the 101 people who responded to the online survey question about health care provision, 25 percent stated their family doctor had asked them directly or indirectly about their caste and 16 percent had experienced the same questioning from a nurse at their doctor's surgery, and 13 percent from a community nurse. A significant number of doctors practising in the NHS [National Health Service] are from overseas (the vast majority from the Indian subcontinent). This indicates a potential for caste discrimination occurring in the health care sector which was highlighted in the focus group cases, one relating to an elderly woman's care worker discriminating against her because of her caste, and the second case about a physiotherapist refusing to treat someone of a low caste.

Recommendation:

The British Medical Association to review the caste issue within its wider equality agenda for patients

Places of Worship

18 percent of survey responses stated they knew the caste system exists because of places of worship specific to particular castes.

In one focus group a man told ACDA about how he had booked his daughter's wedding to take place at a hall in a Sikh gurdwara [a place of worship for a follower of Sikhism, a monotheistic religion founded in India] and a few days before the wedding he was informed by the gurdwara that he could no longer hold the wedding there. He believed this was due to his caste. Another focus group attendee said, "*We had a photo of Guru Ravidas [founder of the Ravidassia movement] at a Sikh temple and they* [the temple priests] *repositioned it in front of the toilets.*" This caused considerable offence to the followers of the Guru in a Sikh place of worship, given that Sikhism is considered an egalitarian faith.

Recommendation:

The Equality and Human Rights Commission to commission an in-depth academic study into the caste system, caste mobility and caste discrimination in the UK, and to research the associated impacts on the health and well-being of victims of caste discrimination.

> *There is clear evidence . . . that the caste system has been imported into the UK . . . and that the associated caste discrimination affects citizens in ways beyond personal choices and social interaction.*

Recommendations for Change

There is clear evidence from the survey and the focus groups that the caste system has been imported into the UK with the Asian diaspora and that the associated caste discrimination affects citizens in ways beyond personal choices and social interaction. There is a danger that if the UK government does not effectively accept and deal with the issue of caste discrimination, the problem will grow unchecked. This will be against the government's values of fairness and equality of treatment so robustly promoted here.

The following recommendations are made to government departments and representative organisations, in the context of the government's policies on encouraging a more cohesive society and the increasing international interest in addressing caste-based discrimination:

1. Government to provide legal protection against caste discrimination for victims (or possible victims), we believe an amendment clause in the Equality Bill 2009 is the right vehicle;

2. Department for children, schools and families to provide guidance to statutory and voluntary organisations and local education authorities (LEAs) for teachers in schools to improve their understanding and skills in recognising caste-based bullying and discrimination.

3. The Department for Work and Pensions, Confederation of British Industry (CBI), and the Trades Union Congress (TUC) to ensure that companies operating in Britain do not inadvertently import caste-based practices, and put monitoring in place to support all workers' and members' rights;

4. The British Medical Association to review the caste issue within its wider equality agenda for patients

5. The Equality and Human Rights Commission to commission an in-depth academic study into the caste system, caste mobility and caste discrimination in the UK, and to research the associated impacts on the health and well-being of victims of caste discrimination.

Women in Russia Face Workplace Discrimination

Elena Novikova

Elena Novikova is a writer for Russia Beyond the Headlines, *a project of the Russian daily* Rossiyskaya Gazeta. *In the following viewpoint, she reports that women in Russia face systematic discrimination. She says that employers often refuse to hire women who have children. The wage gap between men and women in Russia is substantial, she says. Novikova notes that Russia is working on passing gender equality laws, but she says that such laws need to be enforced if they are to be effective.*

As you read, consider the following questions:

1. What evidence did Superjob.ru find in its survey that showed that women were unhappy with life in Russia?
2. What is the gender wage gap in Russia, according to United Nations official data?
3. What is the rate of female participation in parliament in Scandinavia, and how does that compare to the rest of the world, according to Novikova?

Svetlana Fadeyeva, 27, works for a construction company in the Moscow region. Slated for a promotion, she told her boss she was pregnant. The next day, not only was the offer of a promotion rescinded, but her salary was drastically reduced.

Elena Novikova, "Russian Women Regret Being Born Female," *Russia Beyond the Headlines*, March 9, 2011. Reprinted by permission.

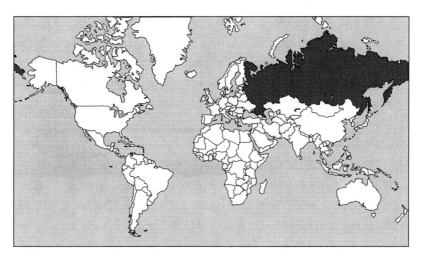

She is currently paid one-third of her former salary, and as the rest of Russia celebrates International Women's Day on March 8 [2011] with a day off, Fadeyeva will work from 9 to 6.

Discrimination Against Women with Children

Unfortunately, Fadeyeva's case is far from the only example of discrimination against pregnant women and women with children. "While I was looking for a job, I had a number of interviews and I was rejected by ten different companies because I had children. Of course nobody tells you a thing like that straight to your face, but when they ask if you have children, you immediately notice how the interviewer's face changes if the answer is yes," said Maria Rybakova, a 32-year-old mother of two who is looking for a job in the banking sector.

It's no wonder that a third of Russian women wish they had been born male. On the eve of International Women's Day, the website Superjob.ru conducted a survey among men and women showing that only 5 percent of women in Russia consider life as a female gratifying. This trend becomes much more evident as age of the participants increases. Among women younger than 24, 26 percent wish to have been born male, while the figure increases to 33 percent among women over 45. A principal reason underlying this frustration is discrimination against women who have or plan to have children. In addition, as one woman surveyed said, men make more money, even if they have exactly the same qualifications for a position.

"Every time I struggle for a more senior position, I regret being born female," said a 27-year-old woman from Orenburg. According to the same survey, 91 percent of men are happy with their gender and don't believe that being female would give them any advantage.

It's no wonder that a third of Russian women wish they had been born male.

The Wage Gap

Several years ago, the United Nations became concerned about discrimination against women in Russia, and that concern was based on valid reasons. According to United Nations official data, the gender wage gap in Russia is between 35 percent and 40 percent. Executive positions are mainly occupied by men, and many organizations that were fighting for women's rights have closed down. The Russian government has only three women in positions of power—Tatyana Golikova, the Minister of Health [and Social Development]; Elvira Nabiullina, the Minister of Economic Development and Yelena Skrynnik, the Minister of Agriculture. Women make up only 13.8 percent of the State Duma, while the Federation Council is less than 5 percent female. The situation is even worse in the regional governments; of 80 regional governors, only two are women.

It seems like the message has finally reached the right person. Pressured by international organizations, Minister of

Sex Segregation by Job in Russia

In responding to the challenges thrown up by economic reform [following the collapse of the Soviet Union in 1990–91], our respondents faced a labour market deeply segregated by sex. This segregation takes place on various levels. In the first instance, the state proscribes the employment of women in particular kinds of work. The impact of this, however, is negligible in comparison to the self-sorting of employees into "gender-appropriate" work, and the strong reinforcement of this through the preferences of employers for a particular gender division of labour. . . . Employers perceive every job to have a "gender profile", but direct discrimination is less common than might be anticipated because employees generally sort themselves into gender-appropriate professions. At the same time, however, the Russian economy is in flux, which means that the gender profile of certain professions is changing. Men have the advantage in this process, because of the widespread assumption that they make superior employees.

Irina Kozina and Elena Zhidkova,
"Sex Segregation and Discrimination
in the New Russian Labour Market,"
in Adapting to Russia's New Labour Market:
Gender and Employment Behaviour, *ed. Sarah Ashwin.*
New York: Routledge, 2006.

Health Golikova announced in a meeting with UN High Commissioner Navanethem [Navi] Pillay that Russia is preparing a gender equality bill. The news came two weeks before the celebration of International Women's Day and has become a symbolic gift to women. Notably, a similar bill was approved by the Duma in 2003, but was later blocked by the government. "There was no gender equality law in Russia until now.

We don't yet have any mechanism to eliminate gender discrimination, although the current legislation contains a number of provisions banning such discrimination."

Passage of the new law has unleashed strong discussion. Many men have spoken against the initiative and fear that the situation could be reversed, while some legal experts remain skeptical and argue that it will have no real impact. The labor code, as well as corresponding articles in the constitution and other legislation, guarantees equality between men and women in Russia. However, such equality is only theoretical, as in real life these laws are ignored and there are currently no mechanisms for enforcement. Without enforcement, a new law won't make any difference. Passing the law is a first step, but the important question to ask is when measures to enforce the law will be implemented.

Executive positions are mainly occupied by men, and many organizations that were fighting for women's rights have closed down.

In Comparison

In Scandinavian countries, women are more highly represented in politics than anywhere else in the world. In Sweden, Denmark, Norway, Iceland and Finland, female participation in parliament ranges between 34 percent and 46 percent, while the global average is just 18 percent.

The first European ministry of gender equality was created in Denmark in 1999. Sweden joined the initiative in 2007, and a year later Spain did the same. A ministry of gender equality also exists in 35 percent of Latin American countries. In 2009, President Hugo Chávez created a ministry of gender equality in Venezuela, saying it was a "gift" to the women of his country.

In Israel, Arabs Face Workplace Discrimination

Jonathan Cook

Jonathan Cook is a British journalist based in Nazareth, Israel. In the following viewpoint, he reports that Arabs are massively underrepresented in Israeli public sector jobs. He says this is caused by systematic workplace discrimination against Arabs. Arabs, he argues, are excluded because they are perceived to be disloyal; as a result, they are excluded from policy-making positions. The fact that Arabs have no voice in government, Cook suggests, contributes to the Arab communities' high levels of poverty and high infant mortality rate.

As you read, consider the following questions:

1. According to Mr. Lashin, what pretext do Israeli employers use to exclude Arabs from jobs?
2. How many Arab workers are there in the Israeli parliament, and what percentage is this?
3. Who is Hatim Kanaaneh?

The unemployed computer engineer Morad Lashin would like to work in Israel's Electricity [Corporation], a large state utility, but said his chances of being recruited are slim. The reasons were set out in graphic form this month [May 2010] when a parliamentary committee revealed that only 1.3

Jonathan Cook, "Arabs Shut Out of Israeli Public Sector," *The National*, May 16, 2010. Reprinted by permission.

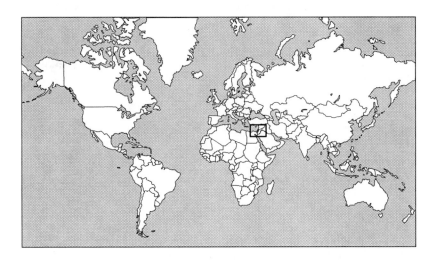

per cent of the company's 12,000 workers are Arab, despite the Arab minority constituting nearly 20 per cent of the population.

Jobless Arab Citizens

The committee's report presents an image of massive under-representation of Arab citizens across most of the public sector, including in government companies and ministries, where the percentage of Arab staff typically falls below two per cent of employees. According to Sikkuy, a group lobbying for greater civic equality, discriminatory hiring policies have left thousands of Arab graduates jobless, even though the government promised affirmative action a decade ago.

Mr Lashin, 30, from Nazareth, said his remaining hope was to find a job in the public sector after a series of short-term contracts in private hi-tech firms. "Everywhere you go, they ask if you have served in the army. Because Arab citizens are exempt, the good jobs are always reserved for Jews." Ali Haider, a co-director of Sikkuy, said: "What kind of example is set for the Israeli private sector when the government consistently finds excuses not to employ Arab citizens too?"

Ahmad Tibi, who heads the parliamentary committee on Arab employment in the public sector, said that even when government bodies appointed Arabs it was invariably in lowly positions. "The absence of Arabs in [senior] roles means that they have no say in the ministries' decision-making processes," he said. The issue of underrepresentation in the public sector was first acknowledged by officials in 2000, when the Fair Representation Law was passed under pressure from Arab political parties.

However, no target was set for the proportion of Arab employees until 2004, when the government agreed that within four years Arabs should comprise 10 per cent of all staff in ministries, state bodies and on the boards of hundreds of government companies. Later the deadline was extended to 2012. The new report found that overall six per cent of the country's 57,000 public sector workers were Arab, only marginally higher than a decade ago.

The committee's report presents an image of massive underrepresentation of Arab citizens across most of the public sector.

Broken Promises

But Mr Tibi noted that the figures were substantially boosted by the large number of "counter staff" in the interior, welfare, health and education ministries employed to provide basic services inside Arab communities. On publication of the report this month, Avishay Braverman, the minorities minister, admitted there was no hope of reaching even the delayed target. He criticised his own government for not setting its sights higher, at 20 per cent representation.

The committee's findings, said Mr Tibi, showed officials had systematically broken their promises on fair representation. He noted that even in the parliament itself there were only six Arab workers out of 439, or 1.6 per cent. "What does it say that in the temple of Israeli democracy there is such rank discrimination?" Similar percentages were found in key government departments, including the prime minister's office, the foreign ministry, the treasury, the housing ministry, and the trade and industry ministry, as well as such state agencies as the Bank of Israel, the Land Administration and the Water Authority.

The Organisation for Economic Co-operation and Development, to which Israel acceded last week, reported last year that 15,000 Arab graduates were either unemployed or forced into work outside their professions, often as teachers. Mr Tibi said he was particularly concerned that there were no Arabs in key roles inside government ministries. "Not by chance are there no senior Arab civil servants, no deputy directors in the ministries, no legal advisers," he said.

He said the absence of Arab policy makers was reflected in the lack of public services and resources made available to Arab communities. Poverty among Arab families is three times higher than among Jewish families. Yousef Jabareen, director of the Dirasat policy centre in Nazareth, said increased recruitment of Arab workers by the government could solve at a stroke two urgent problems: the large pool of Arab graduates who could not find work, and the community's lack of influence on national policy.

"What does it say that in the temple of Israeli democracy there is such rank discrimination?"

Giving Up Hope

He added that discrimination against Arabs was "built into the institutional structure of a Jewish state". The report was received with hostility by some MPs [members of Parliament]. Yariv Levin, chairman of the parliament's House Committee and a member of prime minister Benjamin Netanyahu's Likud Party, said the report was "delusional and ignores the fundamental fact that a significant portion of Israel's Arabs are disloyal to the state".

Saleem Mama, 37, who graduated as an information systems engineer 10 years ago from the prestigious Technion [Israel Institute of Technology] university in Haifa, said he had given up hope of finding regular work in either the private or public sectors. Married with four children, he said he had applied to immigrate to Canada. "I am hopeful that being an Arab won't count against me there." Hatim Kanaaneh, a Harvard-educated doctor who worked as one of the few senior Arab officials in the Israeli health ministry until his resignation in the early 1990s, documented the many battles he faced in the government bureaucracy in his recent book *A Doctor in Galilee*.

Dr Kanaaneh said no Arab had ever risen above the position of sub-district physician he held two decades ago. Although the health ministry had the largest number of Arab employees of any ministry, he said none had ever been appointed to a policy-making position. "In fact, people in the ministry tell me things have gone backwards under recent right-wing governments." He added that the lack of Arab policy makers in government had concrete consequences that damaged the Arab community. When he worked in the health ministry, he noted, the Arab infant mortality rate was twice that of the Jewish population. Two decades later the ratio of Arab to Jewish infant deaths, rather than declining, had increased by a further 25 per cent.

The prejudice faced by educated Arabs seeking employment was highlighted by a survey last November [2009]. It found that 83 per cent of Israeli businesses in the main professions admitted being opposed to hiring Arab graduates. Yossi Coten, director of a training programme in Nazareth, said of 84,000 jobs in the country's hi-tech industries, only 500 were filled by Arab engineers.

Periodical and Internet Sources Bibliography

The following articles have been selected to supplement the diverse views presented in this chapter.

Avert	"HIV/AIDS Stigma and Discrimination," 2011. www.avert.org.
M.V. Lee Badgett, Holning Lau, Brad Sears, and Deborah Ho	"Bias in the Workplace: Consistent Evidence of Sexual Orientation and Gender Identity Discrimination," Williams Institute, June 2007.
Rodney Davis	"Ending HIV/AIDS Discrimination at the Workplace," *Jamaica Gleaner*, October 8, 2006.
Sonia Ghumman and Linda Jackson	"The Downside of Religious Attire: The Muslim Headscarf and Expectations of Obtaining Employment," *Journal of Organizational Behavior*, vol. 31, no. 1, January 2010.
Dan Harris	"Take Advantage of 'China's Rampant Employment Discrimination,'" *ChinaLawBlog*, June 23, 2007. www.chinalawblog.com.
Hartoyo	"Longing for Acceptance, Homosexuals in Indonesia Find Hatred and Discrimination," *Jakarta Globe*, April 16, 2010.
Iran Labor Report	"Iranian Women Labor Woes," June 12, 2010. http://iranlaborreport.com.
Sam Jones	"Asian Caste Discrimination Rife in UK, Says Report," *Guardian*, November 11, 2009.
Divya Talwar	"Caste Discrimination in the UK Could Be Outlawed," BBC News, December 16, 2010. www.bbc.co.uk.
Times of India	"Global Downturn Fuels Discrimination at Workplace," May 17, 2011.

GLOBALVIEWPOINTS

CHAPTER 4

Migrant and Slave Labor

Migrant Domestic Workers Face Slave Labor Conditions in Saudi Arabia

Human Rights Watch

Human Rights Watch (HRW) is an organization dedicated to protecting the human rights of people worldwide. In the following viewpoint, HRW says that migrant domestic workers in Saudi Arabia are excluded from key legal protections and often face slave labor conditions. HRW says that migrant domestic workers can have their wages withheld and their passports taken from them, preventing them from returning to their homeland. HRW also includes testimony from migrant domestic workers discussing the physical, sexual, and psychological abuse they faced.

As you read, consider the following questions:

1. What is the *kafala* system, and why does HRW say that it contributes to abuse of migrant domestic workers?

2. What does HRW say is the primary mechanism for outlining employers' and migrant domestic workers' rights in Saudi Arabia?

3. What is the International Labour Organization's definition of forced or compulsory labor?

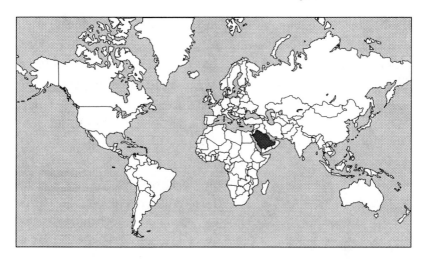

Saudi Arabia's justice system falls far short of international standards and imposes particularly formidable obstacles to migrant domestic workers. Labor laws exclude domestic workers from key protections and immigration policies place migrants at risk through a highly restrictive *kafala* or sponsorship system. Labor-sending governments may have policies regulating minimum standards for their workers abroad, although neither the Philippines, Indonesia, nor Sri Lanka have been able to negotiate a bilateral labor agreement on domestic workers with Saudi Arabia.

Exclusion from Labor Laws

Saudi Arabia applies its interpretation of Sharia (Islamic law) as the governing legal framework. The absence of codified Sharia laws and rules of precedent leaves the government and judiciary significant room for divergent interpretations of the law, and undermines equality before the law. . . .

As it currently stands, Saudi Arabia excludes domestic workers from the provisions of the labor law, leaving them without the protections guaranteed to other workers. These protections include limits to working hours, and restrictions on salary deductions, rest days, and mechanisms for resolving labor disputes. . . .

143

Migrant domestic workers are not only at risk due to their exclusion from labor laws, but also as a result of highly restrictive immigration policies that rely on sponsor-based visas. The kingdom has instituted policies to increase the Saudi component of its workforce that have to date largely failed. These Saudi-ization policies have attempted to limit and control the number of foreign workers and their distribution in various economic sectors. One main strategy has been the *kafala*, or visa sponsorship system, where a worker's visa and legal status is tied to her employer. This system creates a profound power imbalance between employers and workers and imposes tight restrictions on migrant workers' rights.

Most migrant workers arrive in Saudi Arabia on two-year contracts in which their visas are tied to their employer, or "sponsor." The sponsor bears responsibility for the worker's recruitment fees, completion of medical exams, and possession of an *iqama*, or national identity card. The worker must obtain the sponsor's consent to transfer employment or to leave the country (get an "exit visa"). This gives the employer an inordinate amount of power over the worker's ability to change jobs or to return to her country of origin. . . .

Some abusive employers exploit the *kafala* system and force domestic workers to continue working against their will and forbid them from returning to their countries of origin. This legal obstacle, which can result in the arbitrary and unlawful denial of a domestic worker's right to leave Saudi Arabia and return home, is clearly incompatible with article 13 of the Universal Declaration of Human Rights (UDHR), which provides for the right to freedom of movement and the right to return to one's country. In addition to its legal basis under treaty law, the right to return to one's own country has been recognized as a norm of customary international law.

The Saudi Ministry of Labor and the Saudi Human Rights Commission have informed Human Rights Watch that the sponsorship system is under review, and that alternatives are being researched. One proposal is to create three or four large recruitment agencies that would act as sponsors for all migrant workers in the country. This proposal would purportedly address the control that employers have over workers when they also act as immigration sponsors. . . .

If such a proposal was to move forward, these recruitment agencies would wield an enormous amount of power and money. The government would need to regulate and monitor such recruitment agencies rigorously, with clear standards for operating procedures, penalties in case of abuse, and provisions for independent monitoring. One official from a labor-sending country pointed out that a similar system is implemented in Kuwait with poor results. He said, "There are bad aspects. The girl is lost in the agency system. The sponsor may return her to the agency and the agency redeploys her. . . . Why are agencies interested [in this proposal]? Because there is a big bracket of a high-income expat population. The agencies want to exploit that market."

Some abusive employers exploit the kafala *system and force domestic workers to continue working against their will and forbid them from returning to their countries of origin.*

Employment Contracts and Recruitment Practices

In the absence of protection under labor laws, employment contracts are the primary mechanism for outlining both employers' and workers' rights and obligations. Recruitment practices, including initial fees charged to employers and payment of domestic workers' return tickets home, also define certain financial obligations and incentives.

Employment contracts typically stipulate a domestic worker's monthly wage, a two-year period of employment, and the employer's responsibility to provide the domestic worker's meals and accommodation in addition to her salary. These contracts often provide domestic workers a paid one-month vacation every two years. These contracts have many weaknesses. They rarely contain specific information on the conditions of work such as limits on working hours and a detailed description of work responsibilities. These contracts do not have the same types of enforcement mechanisms as protection under labor laws. . . .

Recruitment agencies broker a range of agreements with employers and domestic workers in regard to payment of return tickets. Employers must pay for a domestic worker's air ticket home if she successfully completes her two-year contract or in cases of mistreatment. If a domestic worker terminates her contract early, she may be responsible for paying for own ticket home. Many agencies, both in labor-sending countries and in Saudi Arabia, also offer probation periods in which they provide employers a "replacement maid" within three months if either the employer or the domestic worker decides the arrangement is a poor fit. In such cases, recruitment agencies may pay for the domestic worker's flight home or for a transfer to a new employer, while in other cases they renege on such promises.

One critical area of reform is to protect domestic workers' right to freedom of movement and decent work conditions.

Initial recruitment fees may also profoundly influence the working relationship and the conditions of work. Recruitment agencies charge Saudi employers between 5,000 and 9,000 riyals (US$1300–2340) to hire a domestic worker. When employers bear the responsibility for initial recruitment fees, domestic workers can ideally avoid incurring crushing debts when they migrate. At the same time, many employers feel they have made a significant financial investment and point to their initial payments to justify restrictive measures that prevent a domestic worker from "running away," such as taking her passport, withholding her wages, and physically confining her to the workplace.

Human Rights Watch documented a wide range of abuses against migrant domestic workers in Saudi Arabia.

One critical area of reform is to protect domestic workers' right to freedom of movement and decent work conditions. In addition to outlawing and punishing abusive practices, and educating employers that such treatment likely increases the possibility that a domestic worker will attempt to escape, the Saudi government should also address the concerns of employers who have not committed abuse, for example by introducing an insurance program to recover recruitment fees in cases where domestic workers leave their employment early. . . .

A Wide Range of Abuses

Human Rights Watch documented a wide range of abuses against migrant domestic workers in Saudi Arabia, including deception during recruitment, violations of freedom of movement, physical and sexual abuse, labor exploitation, and double victimization in the criminal justice system. In some cases, domestic workers experienced several of these abuses simultaneously. . . .

Human Rights Watch interviewed 36 women and girl domestic workers whose situations clearly amounted to forced labor, trafficking, slavery, or slavery-like conditions. The following case studies demonstrate how the multiple abuses domestic workers may experience during recruitment and employment can intersect to create these conditions.

No estimates exist regarding the number of such cases in Saudi Arabia, though these egregious abuses likely comprise a minority in comparison to more typical complaints involving delayed payment of wages and overwork. However, many cases of forced labor, trafficking, slavery, or slavery-like conditions are likely never to be identified or reported, due to the worker's isolation, lack of information about her rights, and the employer's ability to repatriate her at will. . . .

Forced Labor

Nour Miyati [an Indonesian domestic worker]:

> This was my third time migrating. The first time I was in Medina for four years. The second time I was in Ta'if for two years. My previous employers were good and provided my full salary.
>
> [The third time in Riyadh], the wife of the employer beat me, she did not work. Every day she beat me. She beat my head, so I would cover it with my hands. She hit my foot with her sharp high heels. Every day she did this until my foot was injured. When I told the husband about his wife's behavior, he also beat me. After she beat my hands and they became swollen, [they made me] wash my hands with . . . one whole cup of bleach. I felt very hurt and had a lot of pain. I never got enough food. After one year, they still had not paid my salary.
>
> I never got a chance to rest, I woke up at 4 a.m., made breakfast for the children, I worked all day without rest. I went to sleep at 3 a.m. So many times I didn't get a chance to sleep at night, I worked around the clock.
>
> My employer had my passport. He is a policeman [a member of the National Guard]. I never got a chance to leave the house. They locked me in from the outside. When I had stayed there for one year, I got a chance to escape, it was a Thursday and I ran out. My condition was bad, my left eye

An Indonesian Domestic Worker Describes Abuse

I wanted to make a new life and try my luck so that my kids would have a different life than their mother.... But I was mistreated by my employers. I began work at 5 a.m. and sometimes finished around 2 or 3 a.m. I never got a day off. The door was always locked. I could never go out alone. I slept in the dining room.

My full salary was deducted [to pay initial recruitment fees] for six and a half months. If I didn't finish [a task quickly], my employer would hit me.... She usually shouted and screamed at me. Once when I was hanging clothes, I had a black eye and my neighbor asked me what happened. My employer had beaten me. That evening the police came and arrested my employers.

—Ati K., Indonesian domestic worker, Kuala Lumpur, Malaysia, February 12, 2010

Human Rights Watch,
Slow Reform: Protection of Migrant Domestic Workers
in Asia and the Middle East, *April 27, 2010. www.hrw.org.*

couldn't see, I was swollen all over. I got a taxi that took me to a police officer.... My employer came to the station and took me back. I refused, I said, "My employer is a bad person." My employer said, "You haven't finished your contract yet, it should be two years."

When I reached the house, they beat me again. They beat my mouth and one tooth fell out [shows scar on her lip]. After that, they locked all the doors, only the bathroom door was unlocked. I was never allowed to go out, not even to throw out the garbage. They didn't let me use the telephone. The situation got very bad. The husband and wife beat me every day, they never gave me medicine.

It got worse after I tried to run away. . . . In the last month I slept in the bathroom. . . . They put tape on my mouth so I couldn't say anything because my employers didn't want the neighbors to know about me.

I didn't escape, I asked [my employer] to take me to the hospital because of my condition. First I had to promise not to tell about their behavior to me. They forced me to stay silent. . . .

[crying] I just worry I cannot work because of my hands. I don't know about my future.

—Nour Miyati (real name used upon request), Indonesian domestic worker, Riyadh, December 5, 2006, and March 11, 2008

Involuntary Work

According to the ILO [International Labour Organization] Convention on Forced Labour, Number 29, forced or compulsory labor "shall mean all work or service which is exacted from any person under the menace of any penalty and for which the said person has not offered himself voluntarily."

The ILO elaborates examples of "menace of penalty" to include: "physical violence against a worker or close associates, physical confinement, financial penalties, denunciation to authorities (police, immigration) and deportation, dismissal from current employment, exclusion from future employment, and the removal of rights and privileges." In the majority of Saudi Arabia forced labor cases we reviewed, employers confined domestic workers to the workplace, including by locking them in from the outside, and withheld their passports, placing them at risk of arrest and punishment if they escaped. As in the case of Nour Miyati, several employers committed or threatened physical violence, and punishments often increased in severity if the domestic worker attempted to escape.

Examples provided by the ILO of the involuntary nature of work include: physical confinement in the work location, psychological compulsion (order to work backed up by a credible threat of a penalty), induced indebtedness (by falsification of accounts, excessive interest charges, etc.), deception about types and terms of work, withholding and nonpayment of wages, and retention of identity documents or other valuable personal possessions.

In the majority of Saudi Arabia forced labor cases we reviewed, employers confined domestic workers to the workplace, including by locking them in from the outside, and withheld their passports.

We documented numerous cases of domestic workers whose experiences met these criteria. Saudi government officials, embassy officials, and domestic workers agree that as a standard practice employers retain domestic workers' passports. Withholding and nonpayment of wages is the most common complaint presented by domestic workers to authorities.... Many labor agents deceive domestic workers about the terms of their work.

Saudi Arabia's requirement that domestic workers obtain their employers' consent in order to receive the necessary clearance ("exit visa") to leave the country greatly increases the risk of forced labor. Human Rights Watch interviewed several domestic workers who were forced to work for months, and in some cases, years, beyond their contracts, because their employers would not allow them to leave the country....

Even if migrant domestic workers have arrived in Saudi Arabia willingly and with full information, they may end up in situations of forced labor. The ILO notes that it is possible for workers to revoke freely given consent: "many victims enter forced labour situations initially of their own accord . . . only to discover later that they are not free to withdraw their labour. They are subsequently unable to leave their work owing to legal, physical or psychological coercion." For example, many domestic workers in Saudi Arabia migrate voluntarily but end up in forced labor situations because their employers do not approve their exit visas to leave the country, withhold months or years of wages, or lock them in the workplace. . . .

Withholding and nonpayment of wages is the most common complaint presented by domestic workers to authorities.

Slavery and Slavery-Like Conditions

Haima G. [a Filipina domestic worker]

I am 17 years old, from Mindanao. I have, finished three years of high school. I was 15 when I left. I wanted to help my family. My cousins fooled me into coming here, my parents thought I'd be with them, but actually they were far away. . . . They really fooled me, if I had known what Saudi Arabia is like, I wouldn't have come, not even if they gave me millions *[eyes filling with tears]*. My father didn't ask my permission, I had to go. I thought I would babysit children and go to school at the same time. I did not know I would be a full-time maid, cleaning. I didn't even know my wages.

They took me to an agency [in Saudi Arabia] where they trick people. I stayed in the agency for one week. I had to work in five houses in one week. One day the agent said he would take me to his sibling's house. He was the only one there. He started holding me, kissing me. He said he would marry me, that he would call my family, and give me money. He asked how old I am. I said, "I am 24." He said, "I know you are not 24." He was kissing me. I was crying, "don't do this to me, I am Muslim."

When we went back to the agency, my true employer, the one I would be sold to, was there. I didn't want to go back to the agency because he touched me all over and kissed me and I thought maybe he would rape me. The true employer got me and brought me to the house. He said, "Be good so I don't send you back [to the agency]."

After a while, the employer started showing some affection for me. He called me into his bedroom. He said, "I want to tell you how I got you from the agency." He said, "I bought you for 10,000 riyals." That is when I found out I had been sold. . . .

He said, "I will do something to you, but don't tell anyone." He injected me with something, but I don't know what it was. He said, "If you don't want to go back to the agency, you better stay here." I felt dizzy and feverish after the injection. He really threatened me, "Don't tell madam."

[gets quiet] I felt there was no hope. The employer raped me. The lady employer was noticing something about me, that I was exhausted. The employer raped me many times. Not in my bedroom, because I locked the door, but around the house.

[crying] I thought, I can't take it anymore, I stayed in my bedroom for two days, I had a phone in my room because they are rich, and they called me. I told everything to madam. Madam also cried. Madam said, "We can't do anything about it, I know he's really bad, every time that he is drunk, he does bad things."

I said, "I want to go to the Philippines." The whole family, madam, the employer, they didn't want me to go. They locked the doors and the gates. One night, still in February, there was a party. I thought, now I can escape, and I prayed and prayed. I saw that the gate was unlocked . . . [and escaped to the embassy.]

I went to the [police] station with an embassy official. After that, they brought the employer to Sulaimaniya, he was put in prison. They brought me to the SSWA [a shelter run by the Ministry of Social Affairs]. I was there for one month. After four days in the SSWA, the employer who was in prison came to the SSWA and we had another interview. He asked how much money I wanted [for an out of court settlement]. I said, "I don't want money. I want him to suffer and go to jail."

I don't want to go home feeling empty like the others, without bringing money, even just one riyal. I cry, how long will I have to wait here in the embassy? I have been here nine months.

One day, they told me the case was unsuccessful [and I will be sent to deportation to return home.]

I was treated really badly. It is as if I don't have a family and I am not a human being.

—Haima G., Filipina domestic worker, 17 years old, Riyadh, December 7, 2006

We found that the combination of the high recruitment fees paid by Saudi employers and the power granted them by the kafala *system . . . made some employers feel entitled to exert "ownership" over a domestic worker.*

Situations of slavery are distinguished by exercising powers of ownership over a human being. The Elements of Crimes, which elaborates how the Rome Statute (establishing the International Criminal Court) should be interpreted, provides the most contemporary definition of enslavement: "The perpetrator exercised any or all of the powers attaching to the right of ownership over one or more persons, such as purchasing, selling, lending or bartering such a person or persons, or by imposing on them a similar deprivation of liberty." It adds that such deprivation of liberty may, in some circumstances, include exacting forced labour or otherwise reducing a person to a servile status as defined in the Supplementary Convention on the Abolition of Slavery.

Haima G.'s situation amounts to trafficking and conditions of slavery, as relatives deceived Haima G. about her promised job abroad, her agent sexually harassed her, and her employer threatened to return her to her abusive agent if she complained. Her employer sexually assaulted her, retained her passport, and locked her in the workplace so that she could not escape.

We found that the combination of the high recruitment fees paid by Saudi employers and the power granted them by the *kafala* system to control whether a worker can change employers or exit the country made some employers feel entitled to exert "ownership" over a domestic worker. According to recruitment agents and embassy officials interviewed by Human Rights Watch, employers typically pay approximately 6,000–9,000 riyals ($1,560–2,340) to hire a domestic worker. The employer's reference to "buying" Haima G. for 10,000 riyals because he had paid a recruitment fee illustrates the sense of ownership that creates slavery-like conditions.

Germany Is Cracking Down on Migrant Slave Labor in Chinese Restaurants

Andreas Ulrich

Andreas Ulrich is a journalist with the German newspaper Spiegel. *In the following viewpoint, he reports that Chinese cooks in some restaurants in Germany are treated as slave labor. He says that Chinese cooks work long hours often for much less pay than they were promised, and if they complain, they may be deported or even beaten. Ulrich says the German government is trying to crack down on those who exploit these laborers. However, Ulrich notes, many government officials seem indifferent to the Chinese cooks' plight.*

As you read, consider the following questions:

1. What were some problems with the food in the restaurant where he worked, according to Zhao Zhen?

2. How many Asian restaurants does Ulrich say there are in Germany, and how many Chinese people work in them?

3. How many days and hours have the cooks represented by Welke each worked at minimum, according to Ulrich?

Andreas Ulrich, "Chinese Restaurants Accused of Human Trafficking," *Spiegel*, August 20, 2009. Reprinted by permission.

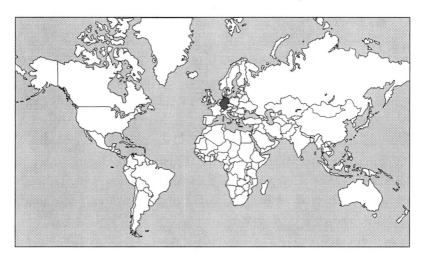

Aijun G. wanted to take a sick day. "You can take a break when you have cancer!" his boss screamed. Then, he claims, his boss added: "What would happen to me anyway, even if I beat you to death?" He then attacked his employee with a chair, threatened him with the broken neck of a bottle and shouted, "If you go to the police, I'll stab you!"

Large Profits, Low Risk

That was the pinnacle so far of Aijun G.'s working life in Germany. The rest of the time, he had to cook, wash dishes, mop the floor and clean stove exhaust hoods for up to 12 hours a day in an Asian restaurant in Speyer, a small city in southwestern Germany. For his labors, he was paid a maximum of €900 ($1,270) a month—far less than promised when he was recruited back in China.

By the time Aijun G. tried to go home sick, it was clear to him that his dream of returning home from Germany a wealthy man would never materialize. He has since pressed criminal charges and sued for the wages he wasn't paid. A court recently dismissed the criminal proceedings for assault in exchange for the payment of a fine. The case in the labor court is continuing.

It's impossible to say whether Aijun G. will ever be paid. But for law enforcement authorities, at least, the case of the mistreated cook in Speyer has proven valuable. Until this case, police investigations into Chinese restaurants in Germany tended to be focused on widespread protection payment rackets. Now investigators have their sights on a very different kind of criminal activity: a sort of 21st-century slave trade.

There are hundreds of people from China being lured to the West. Once they get here, they are sometimes brutally exploited. It's a type of human trafficking that offers large profits and low risk. Smuggling organizations disguised as employment agencies earn big, while restaurant owners profit from their employees' low wages.

The victims are people like Zhao Zhen [name changed by *Spiegel*], 36, from Jiangsu Province in eastern China. Together with his wife, two children, parents and parents-in-law, Zhao lived in a simple mud brick house with a dirt floor. He kept chickens and grew vegetables on his property because the €100 a month he earned as a cook in China wasn't enough to feed the whole family.

There are hundreds of people from China being lured to the West. Once they get here, they are sometimes brutally exploited.

At an employment agency, he was told he could cook in Germany and earn 10 times as much money. A frugal man like Zhao would be able to put away as much as €25,000 in the course of four years—a literal fortune compared to what he earned in China. The prospect of being able to pay for his children's education and buy the family a bigger house was so enticing that Zhao agreed to go.

But first, he had to pay the equivalent of €10,000 to cover agency fees, paperwork and travel costs. Zhao borrowed money from the bank and from relatives and friends. Then he signed two contracts—one in Chinese and one in German. He couldn't read the German one, of course, but the agent assured him it was only a formality for entry into Germany. Zhao also applied for a passport.

When he left for his new life in Europe, he packed eight pairs of work shoes, 15 shirts and several pairs of pants. He knew the cost of living in Europe was a lot higher than at home. Zhao traveled first by bus to Nanjing and then on to Beijing, where he boarded a plane for the first time in his life. His new boss was waiting for him at the airport in Berlin and took Zhao's passport from him right away. They didn't talk much.

"If you don't work, we'll send you back to China."

Thirteen-Hour Shifts, Seven Days a Week

In the restaurant kitchen, his boss taught him how to cook Chinese food to Germans' tastes. "The quality was worse than back home, and it didn't taste as good," Zhao said. Vegetables left unfinished by customers were cooked into sweet and sour soup, and leftover meat had to be washed and served again the next day. "I wouldn't have eaten it," Zhao says.

He wasn't allowed to anyway. During his shifts, which ran seven days a week from 10 a.m. to 11 p.m., he was only given rice, noodles and Chinese cabbage to eat. He slept on a mattress in the laundry room. At the end of the first month, his boss gave him €300. "He kept the rest, supposedly as a security deposit so I wouldn't run away," Zhao said. When he complained to the agency, he was given a terse reply: "If you don't work, we'll send you back to China."

More than One Hundred Restaurants Raided

There are around 10,000 Asian restaurants in Germany, and the demand for cheap cooks is correspondingly large. As many as 4,000 Chinese people work in Germany's Asian restaurants. And every year, between 700 and 800 more Chinese cooks are issued work permits, which must be approved by the German federal labor office's International Placement [Service] (ZAV).

To encourage cultural diversity in Germany, an agreement with China allows selected specialty cooks to work in Germany for up to four years. In order to qualify, they must have abilities German cooks don't.

Officials at ZAV check whether the strict terms of the agreement have been fulfilled before issuing a work permit. The cooks must present credentials and demonstrate an ability to speak German or English. The employer must pay the travel costs to Germany and back; and working hours, pay and vacation entitlement have to correspond to the respective pay rate generally observed in the industry.

Around two dozen so-called educational institutions in China send specialty cooks to Germany and they are regulated by the state-run China International Contractors Association. But German authorities fear that many of these institutions aren't what they claim to be.

They have to pay their own travel costs and a secret supplementary contract leaves them with virtually no rights.

Last year [2008] the German Foreign Ministry temporarily barred many of these Chinese institutions from the visa process because cooks' credentials had clearly been forged. Meanwhile, ZAV officials are also aware that the paperwork they process doesn't always correspond to the reality in the kitchen. "We follow up on evidence of violations," said ZAV's Beate Raabe.

Such abuse starts with the cooks often having to pay much higher commissions than agreed upon by the two countries.

In addition, they have to pay their own travel costs and a secret supplementary contract leaves them with virtually no rights.

The cook, one of these contracts reads, should "work diligently, hard and perseveringly," "not gamble," and listen to "the boss' advice." The cook must also be clear about the fact that work "in German kitchens (requires) good physical strength," and that the employee is required not just to cook but also to "wash dishes, clean floors and stove hoods" and much more. Anyone unprepared for this work should refrain from signing in the first place, the contract states. In addition, the contract cannot be terminated.

The employer is obligated only to take care of work and residence permits and pay a salary, insurance and taxes. A €1,500 deposit is withheld from the first wages, and the employer determines working hours and when vacations can be taken. The contract also reads, however, that the employer will "not deliberately injure (the cook) physically or psychologically."

Finally, both employer and employee pledge "under no circumstances (to disclose) details about the content of the contract to third parties." The official employment contract, this second contract continues, is "only for use in the visa application," and has "no binding power."

Yang Wang [name changed by *Spiegel*] also signed two contracts, one for the authorities and another one that virtually made her a serf. Also from Jiangsu Province, she paid about €9,000 to two different agencies. In exchange, she received cooking courses that turned her from a simple cook into a certified specialist in just a few days' time.

She flew to Hamburg, where her new boss picked her up at the airport. Work started the very next day. She toiled 11 to 13 hours a day and at the end of the month received €680 in cash—far less than she had been promised.

A Case of Slave Labor in the United States

Ravi was among hundreds of workers lured to the United States from India by an oil rig construction company operating in the Gulf Coast. Lacking skilled welders and pipe fitters to help rebuild after Hurricane Katrina struck the area in 2005, the company brought Ravi and others from India on H-2B visas [for temporary workers], promising them permanent visas and residency. But, the promises were false. Instead, Ravi was forced to live with 23 other men in a small room with no privacy and two toilets. The camp was lined with barbed wire and security guards, so no one on the outside knew Ravi's whereabouts. The company charged so much for food and a bunk bed that Ravi was unable to send any money home or repay the money he borrowed for his travel expenses to the United States. When the workers began organizing to protest their working conditions, the company began arbitrary firings and private deportations of the protest leaders. Those who remained filed a class action lawsuit and applied for TVPA [Trafficking Victims Protection Act] immigration services.

US State Department, "Victims' Stories,"
Trafficking in Persons Report 2011, *2011. www.state.gov.*

Fighting Back

Bernhard Welke, 47, a lawyer in . . . the eastern German state of Saxony-Anhalt, used to make his living primarily through traffic accidents, contract law and other civil disputes. But that changed two years ago, when he stumbled across a Chinese cook who told him about his suffering.

Welke now represents more than 60 Chinese clients who feel they've been deceived and exploited by their bosses and the employment agencies, and he carries out labor-related lawsuits throughout Germany. The cases, however, sometimes end up superfluous when immigration authorities deport the cooks who are trying to defend themselves. When these employees lose their jobs, they are quickly stripped of their work and residence permits as well. And that, in fact, is the easiest solution for the restaurant owners, who then don't have to worry about any further trouble.

In Welke's experience, many restaurant owners make a point of establishing good contacts with the relevant authorities, winning themselves preferential treatment when it comes to filling out the residency papers that have to be issued after the cooks arrive and before they can begin work.

According to Welke, one Chinese restaurant owner in the western state of Rhineland-Palatinate, for example, even gloated about his close acquaintance with a woman working for the immigration authorities. Welke says he sometimes gets the impression officials would rather cozy up to restaurant owners than concern themselves with the problems cooks face.

That was true in Aijun G.'s case in Speyer as well. A contractual disclaimer often lets employers get away scot-free. According to this clause, entitlement to the payment of overtime hours expires if not claimed within a certain period. The burden of proof lies with the employee.

Welke says he sometimes gets the impression officials would rather cozy up to restaurant owners than concern themselves with the problems cooks face.

The cooks Welke represents have had to work at least six days a week, clocking up as much as 65 to 94 hours of labor. In most cases, they earn no more than €600 a month, which is handed to them in cash. Very often no payroll accounting is even done. They had almost no contact to the outside world. If they wanted to use a mobile phone, they had to go through their bosses, who could thus monitor employees' calls. Anyone who defied the regime risked facing what happened in one case in the western German city of Osnabrück—a visit from a gang of thugs.

Almost all of the cooks had their passports taken away immediately after their arrival. According to Welke's information, the passports are then sometimes used by other people to enter into casinos or to transfer money to China. Investigators also believe people from China may be smuggled into the European Union using these passports.

For Chinese restaurants in Germany, these kitchen slaves are a lucrative business. If a cook is entitled to gross earnings of €1,900 a month for a 39-hour work week, but instead works a 78-hour week for €600, then the restaurant owner saves €3,200 a month.

Australian Consumers Should Put Pressure on Slave Labor Employers

Kelly Griffin

Kelly Griffin is a writer and journalist whose work has been published in Australia and the United Kingdom. In the following viewpoint, Griffin argues that migrant outworkers, who work in their own homes, face slavery-like conditions in Australia. Griffin says that outworkers are paid very little and are exploited by subcontractors and middlemen. As a result, she says, outwork is often more dangerous and more exploitive than factory work. She concludes that Australian consumers can help to change these practices by avoiding products made by exploited labor.

As you read, consider the following questions:

1. According to TCFUA, how many home workers are there in Australia, and what are their hours and pay like?
2. Why do outworkers suffer more injuries than factory workers, according to Quinlan and Mayhew?
3. What part of the Ethical Clothing Code of Practice have most retailers signed, and what part have they not signed?

Kelly Griffin, "Worker Exploitation in Our Own Backyard," *Aduki*, December 18, 2007. Reprinted by permission.

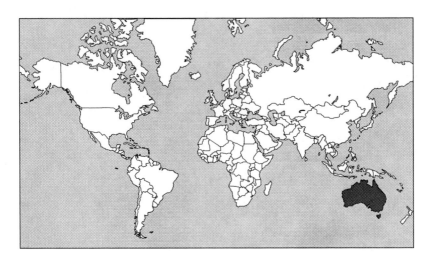

Thousands of straining Asian women of all ages are packed into murky factories, bent over archaic sewing machines, slaving away, quite literally, making countless garments, textiles and footwear hour upon hour, for as little as $2 a day.

Exploitation at Home

You've probably seen the appalling footage and read about the exploitative slave-labour industry in foreign countries, in far off places. What you may not know, however, is that these unethical practices are actually taking place in our own backyard, and are being endorsed by local retailers, designers and even suppliers of our school uniforms.

Where Australian sweatshops were a thing of the 70s, 80s and 90s, these days money-hungry manufactures are employing and exploiting home workers (also known as outworkers). Home workers typically do the same tasks as sweatshop workers and endure similar unethical working conditions, the only difference is that employers save money on the costs of employing individuals full-time, space and facilities by having their labourers work from their own homes.

According to the Textile Clothing and Footwear Union of Australia (TCFUA) there are about 300,000 home workers in

Australia who work up to 15 or more hours per day, for as little as $2–$3 an hour, seven days a week.

Most Australian home workers, also known as outworkers, are first generation migrant women who end up slaving away (quite literally) in our textile, clothing and footwear industries, for myriad reasons. Some do it because they have a history of working in slave labour, others because it allows them to work at home while caring for young children or elderly family members, or because this form of employment is one of a very small, select few jobs in Australia where being unable to speak the local tongue is not an issue.

Home-based work is often cash in hand, off the records and therefore unregulated labour. According to an article published by youth activist organisation ActNow, home workers "have no or minimal entitlements (such as holidays, sick leave, etc.), work in conditions that risk their health and safety, and work long hours to meet unrealistic deadlines."

These unethical practices are actually taking place in our own backyard and are being endorsed by local retailers, designers and even suppliers of our school uniforms.

Outwork Worse than Factory Work

In 1998 Professor Michael Quinlan and Claire Mayhew of the University of New South Wales compiled a comprehensive survey, which compared the working conditions of 100 factory-based workers with 100 home workers. The findings showed that outworkers suffered more injuries than factory workers, presumably because home workers worked for longer hours "and that in turn was a response to very low rates of pay and the incentive payment system they were under," Quinlan explained. He added, "We found that typically clothing outworkers were being paid between 25 per cent and one-third of the going award rate; as a result, to try to maintain a standard of living, they were working longer hours. These low rates of pay were directly due to the subcontracting system and the commercial pressures that resulted from the subcontracting system."

This report also alarmingly demonstrated that while very few factory-based workers reported experiencing occupational violence, 49 per cent of outworkers were exposed to verbal abuse, 23 per cent to threats and 7 per cent had experienced physical assault. Mayhew and Quinlan noted that, "The occupational health and safety of outworkers was unequivocally and significantly worse than that of factory-based textile, clothing and footwear workers," and that there was "considerable occupational violence involving the predominantly migrant women who work as clothing outworkers."

Quinlan said this report debunked the myth, "that the home is a safe and family friendly" place to work because these people were actually being assaulted in their own homes. He elaborates, "If somebody tries to assault you in a factory, it is a very visible act in front of lots of witnesses but you can be assaulted at home and no one will see it." These people, because they are often recently arrived immigrants, are not going to speak out and report these sorts of issues particularly because they fear if they do they will never get any future work.

"The occupational health and safety of outworkers was unequivocally and significantly worse than that of factory-based textile, clothing and footwear workers."

According to an article published in the *Green Left Weekly* in 2002, retail companies deliberately employ sub-contractors, aka middlemen, to employ outworkers, thereby distancing themselves directly from being responsible for the conditions that outworkers endure. Quinlan was quoted in the *Sunday Telegraph* in 2001 saying, "What happens is that as these workplaces proliferate and move people out of factories where inspectors can check conditions, you end up with a situation that is impossible to police. The whole system basically becomes unenforceable."

While it's the big companies that dominate the industry that established and maintains this exploitative production chain, the middlemen further perpetuate the problem by trying to cut corners and make their own personal profits along the way. Sub-contractors usually make their profits by paying outworkers far less per piece than the subcontractor receives from the business for manufacturing the item, or by forcing outworkers to work long hours in crowded or unhealthy conditions to meet unrealistic demands. Sometimes children help after school and on weekends to meet these unworkable deadlines.

As individuals we can make a difference by becoming aware of which labels exploit, and alternatively which labels support their workers.

There are laws in Australia to prevent worker exploitation, but the problem is enforcing these laws because outworkers are often isolated and are not usually registered employees.

According to a Victorian Parliament report . . . compiled by the Family and Community Development Committee in 2002, there are two acts that aim to protect workers: the *Occupational Health and Safety Act*, which is the prevention act, and the *Accident Compensation Act*. The report stated however that despite these acts, the reality is that in both there is quite a lot of uncertainty and ambiguity as to coverage. In some cases people may be covered and may not be aware that they are, and in other cases they may not be covered, and this is one of the problems. Mayhew and Quinlan noted that this complication was due to the complex employment relationships whereby it was sometimes difficult to tell who was the employer (accountable for the conditions) and who was the employee.

Public Pressure Can Cause Change

As public pressure and awareness gradually increase, changes to the outworker industry are slowly coming about, reports ActNow. In 2002 the [Australian] Retailers [Association's] Ethical Clothing Code of Practice was introduced, making retailers, as well as manufactures, responsible for the fair treatment of outworkers. However, this code is voluntary, so although a number of Australian companies have signed part one of the code (agreeing to show their record[s]), very few have signed part two (agreeing to pay minimum wages and provide safe work conditions, etc.).

Yet there is hope. As individuals we can make a difference by becoming aware of which labels exploit, and alternatively which labels support their workers. Think critically before you purchase new clothes, about how they were made and under what conditions.

In Britain, Internships Have Features in Common with Slave Labor

Tom Rawstorne

Tom Rawstorne is a journalist who writes for the United Kingdom newspaper the Daily Mail. *In the following viewpoint, he says that many firms in the United Kingdom expect interns to work for free in exchange for experience. Rawstorne argues that this practice is unjust and that it violates Britain's minimum wage laws. Rawstorne further notes that internships favor well-to-do individuals, who can afford to work for free for a time to gain experience. Those who are less well-off, he said, are effectively locked out of entry-level employment and a career in their chosen field.*

As you read, consider the following questions:

1. What statistics does Rawstorne cite to show that those who graduated in 2008 and after faced difficulty finding employment?

2. Why does Rawstorne say that there has been a huge growth in "soft" degrees?

3. What was the philosophy behind offering internships to undergraduates, according to Rawstorne?

Tom Rawstorne, "The Slave Labour Graduates: Cynical Firms Are Forcing Thousands of High Flyers to Work for Nothing—Or Even Making Them Pay for the Privilege," *Daily Mail*, March 4, 2010. Reprinted by permission.

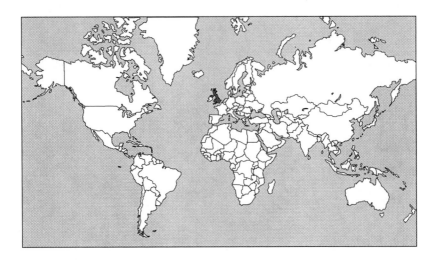

Across London, the cream of a generation take their first steps in the world of work. At a prestigious PR [public relations] firm, a 22-year-old with a 2:1 [second-class honors] from one of the country's leading universities, is given the task of directing incoming phone calls for eight hours a day.

Work Without Pay

For her trouble, she will be paid not a penny—not even her travel costs to and from the office or the cost of her lunch. Hungry, she helps herself from the staff biscuit tin, but finds herself publicly scolded like a naughty child.

Elsewhere in the capital, another graduate, Mark, a 22-year-old with a first-class philosophy degree and a master's in art theory, is beginning his first day at a plush art gallery in the West End.

He's already racked up thousands of pounds in debts from his studies and tentatively asks his boss if he could clarify what remuneration he will be receiving for his work in their marketing department.

'We can't afford to pay you,' he is told. 'Not even your expenses. I'm very sorry, but we don't have the budget.' The words echo around the office, all black marble and £2,000 leather sofas.

Then there's the experience of Sam, a 23-year-old with a master's degree from Durham [University].

'I'm terrified that any refusal will lead to a terrible reference,' she says.

'So I never refuse to do anything, no matter how absurd or mundane. In the meantime I am effectively paying, since I have to pay for my own travel expenses, to have my dignity and self-respect peeled away. Even prostitutes get paid for their services—we have to pay our punters [that is, the brothel patrons].'

Welcome to the world of the graduate intern—a world of unpaid work where the academically gifted are treated like schoolchildren on work experience, the promise of a 'proper' job dangled carrot-like in front of their noses.

"Even prostitutes get paid for their services—we have to pay our punters."

Indeed, so desperate are university leavers for employment that not only are they willing to work for free but some are actually paying thousands of pounds for the privilege.

They know that, at a time when one million under-25s are unemployed, when it comes to getting a job, then the fuller the CV [curriculum vitae] the better.

Only the Well-Off Advance

The problem is, of course, that it is a route that only the well-off can even consider.

Having racked up record levels of debt during their studies, for the majority, spending three months as an unpaid intern simply isn't an option.

'Whatever happened to getting ahead on merit?' asks Alex Try, a 23-year-old graduate who is campaigning to highlight the way in which internships are being abused.

'There is no regulation, there is no system of best practice. Employers are simply taking us for a ride.'

That graduates have no option but to go along on that ride is because the 'Class of the Credit Crunch' [referring to the tightening of credit in 2008 as a result of a financial crisis] are suffering in an unprecedented manner.

Of those who graduated in the summer of 2008, eight per cent were still unemployed six months later. That represents an increase of 44 per cent over the previous year.

Over the past 12 months [2009–2010], the situation has deteriorated still further with statistics showing unemployment rising fastest among 18- to 24-year-olds who have degrees.

Of those who graduated in the summer of 2008, eight per cent were still unemployed six months later.

One in ten graduates is now believed to be unable to find work while even those lucky enough to find paid employment are having to take jobs that match neither their aspirations nor qualifications.

As for the outlook for this year's crop of graduates, that is equally bleak. Analysts warn that any vacancies that do emerge will be swamped by those who have failed to find jobs in previous years.

That today's students find themselves in such a parlous situation is due to the fact that the recession has affected employment patterns in different ways than previous downturns.

During the eighties and early nineties, it was industrial workers who bore the brunt of large-scale job cuts. This time, employers have chosen to reduce their workforces by halting recruitment. At the same time there has been a big increase in the actual number of graduates out there looking for work.

Last year PricewaterhouseCoopers—the biggest graduate recruiter—received almost 20,000 applications for 1,000 positions.

Microsoft closed applications for its graduate scheme two months early after receiving 5,000 applications for just 25 posts. John Lewis, meanwhile, had 250 candidates chasing each graduate vacancy on offer.

More Graduates, Fewer Jobs

In 2009, a record 400,000 students graduated from British universities, the unprecedented numbers a direct result of [former prime minister] Tony Blair's Utopian dream of opening university education to all.

For the last decade school leavers, who would previously have gone straight into a job, have been encouraged to ignore their academic weaknesses and sign up for a course. Any course.

As a result there has been a huge growth in so-called 'soft' degrees, the worth of which was being questioned even while the economy was buoyant.

In a recession, the fact that the number of media studies courses on offer across the country outnumbers those in aeronautical engineering five to one looks even more wrongheaded.

Of course, these students were encouraged to take up such courses by claims that when they graduated they would be able to command better-paid jobs.

Over a working lifetime, the government claimed, a degree could be worth an extra £400,000 when compared with the average British wage. Even before the economy collapsed those figures did not stand up to scrutiny.

Not only does it depend on where the degree is from but the boost to any future earnings also depends hugely on the subject. While a math degree can bring significant material advantage, it has been estimated that a man with an arts degree may only benefit to the tune of £22,000.

When the cost of a modern-day degree is taken into account (the average debt a student leaves with is £15,700—a sum that will, on average, take 11 years to repay) it is easy to understand the disillusionment felt by this new wave of graduates as they discover that, in 21st-century Britain, a degree on its own is not enough.

It is a situation that Mark, now working in the London art gallery, found himself in when he finished his master's last year.

'I am keen to work in the arts world and so applied for any vacancies that I could find,' he says.

'But after a while, it became clear that I simply wasn't going to get anywhere. All my friends were doing internships so it seemed like the only option. I applied for about 30 of them and, when the gallery said they had a vacancy, I felt extremely lucky.'

While internships have long been popular in America, it is only in recent years that they have become increasingly important in Britain. What they are in practice is something of a moveable feast.

Generally lasting anywhere between one week and three months, they are supposed to be an opportunity for a potential employee to experience working at a firm or a charity (or, indeed, in the political system).

Previously these internships were generally offered to undergraduates who would typically fill the posts during long summer holidays. The idea was that it would give them a flavour of an industry while building up a relationship with a future employer. In this way the system was mutually beneficial.

Increasingly, however, interns are now fully fledged graduates like Mark who cannot find work and who feel that the only way to do so is to gain extra experience by working for free.

The hope is that if they impress they may be offered a full-time job with the company for whom they are doing the internship or, at the very least, bolster their CV. In theory it sounds not unreasonable. After all, getting ahead in one's chosen profession has long entailed personal sacrifice.

Increasingly, however, interns are now fully fledged graduates like Mark who cannot find work and who feel that the only way to do so is to gain extra experience by working for free.

However, there are growing concerns that the formalisation of the internship as the first step on the career ladder may not only distort the labour market but make certain jobs inaccessible to the less well-off.

First, there is evidence that recession-hit employers are using the system to reduce their costs. Paid jobs that graduates would have previously gone into are being scrapped and replaced by internships. These positions are then filled, permanently, with an ever-changing rota of unpaid interns.

Graduates Being Exploited

'What we have found is that thousands and thousands of graduates are doing these unpaid work placements and, as a result, these entry-level jobs are drying up,' says Mr Try, who has set up a website called Interns Anonymous to highlight the harsh reality of life as a graduate intern.

'Companies aren't willing to take chances and pay £16,000 or £18,000 on a project assistant or a campaign assistant. Instead they are looking to graduates to provide free labour while holding out the promise of a job. The problem is that they rarely seem to deliver on that promise.'

Having graduated with a 2:1 in history from Manchester University, Mr Try spent three months as an intern working at a Westminster think tank. There was no job at the end of his time there.

Internships and Workers' Rights in the United States

Convinced ... many unpaid internships violate minimum wage laws, officials in Oregon, California and other states have begun investigations. ...

Many regulators say that violations are widespread, but that it is unusually hard to mount a major enforcement effort because interns are often afraid to file complaints. Many fear they will become known as troublemakers in their chosen field, endangering their chances with a potential future employer.

Steven Greenhouse,
"The Unpaid Intern, Legal or Not,"
New York Times, April 2, 2010.

He adds: 'We know people who have worked for month after month and been told that at the end of it there will be a job. One woman commuted in from Slough to London every day for seven months, and spent thousands of pounds doing so, only finally to be told that there wasn't a job after all.'

Another point to make is that these interns can only claim a job seekers' allowance at the same time if they have been on benefits and out of work for a full six months. Not many fit that bill so soon after graduating. Further, they cannot claim housing benefit if they [are] living at their parents' home, as many are.

The impression that graduates are being exploited is bolstered by a growing number of organisations offering companies a never-ending supply of graduates. They charge about £500 for each intern provided.

One such company extols the virtues of internships as a 'low-cost' way of finding staff that allows firms the chance to cut human resources costs—'full-time employees require salaries, bonuses, payroll taxes, benefits, etc.'

'What we have found is that thousands and thousands of graduates are doing these unpaid work placements and, as a result, these entry-level jobs are drying up.'

The question of payment aside, the second concern relating to internships is the way in which they restrict access to the few real jobs that are out there.

A graduate spending three months in an unpaid internship, generally in London, will need to support themselves financially during that period. That is alright if they have wealthy parents or access to savings, but for the majority it is an economic impossibility.

Consider the situation that 22-year-old Harriet Pomfret finds herself in. Last summer she completed a degree in physics and astrophysics at York University, during which she racked up debts of £18,000.

She comes from a modest background (her mother is a cook in a residential home) and she had assumed that on graduating she would be able to walk into a well-paid job in either the defence or the nuclear industries.

But eight months on from her graduation and things have hardly panned out as planned. Instead of embarking on a financially rewarding career at the cutting edge of science, Harriet is back living at home.

Having claimed £50-a-week Jobseeker's Allowance for three months, she is now working as a part-time shop assistant in a health and beauty store. For her two days' work a week, she is paid just £80.

Of course, she says, she'd love to do an internship. But how on earth could she afford it?

'It is something I have considered but at the moment my priority is to earn enough money to live on,' says Harriet, who is from Clitheroe, Lancashire.

'I don't have any savings and I can't save any money at the moment, so an internship is out of the question.'

'Anyway,' she adds, 'the reason I did a degree was to get a job—not so that I could go and work for free for someone.'

If it looks like work and smells like work, then it should be paid as work.

Graduates Should Be Paid

It is a point echoed by Jonathan Black, director of Oxford University's careers service.

He says he is regularly approached by companies who want to sell their services to students—charging them up to £8,000 to set up internships in the City and the media.

(Recently there has been a spate of charity auctions of internships. The NSPCC [National Society for the Prevention of Cruelty to Children] recently "sold" a month-long placement at Christie's, the auction house, for £4,600, while a week at Rothschild investment bank went for nearly £1,500).

Clearly, such sums can only be afforded by a privileged minority. More to the point, Mr Black argues that graduates should be going straight into paid employment.

It is for this reason that the university refused to back a new government scheme to fund thousands more graduate internships.

'We didn't support it because we think that internships are for undergraduates,' says Mr Black. 'Once you have graduated it is time for a job, simple as that.'

Of course, many would argue that an internship, to all intents and purposes, is a job—and as such should be paid as one. Under legislation brought in by Labour, the national minimum wage has to be paid to anyone defined as a 'worker'.

While that definition is open to interpretation, it means that if it looks like work and smells like work, then it should be paid as work. In the eyes of the law, labelling a position an 'internship' does not make it exempt from payment.

The trouble is that few graduates working in these positions are ever likely to complain about their treatment.

It is something that Mark Watson, a freelance television producer, knows only too well.

All too often he has seen young graduates desperate for work exploited by production companies and the like. On a number of occasions he has helped individuals persuade their employers to pay them the proper wage that they are due. But generally, he says, they do not want to rock the boat.

'Even when they have a rough time they look back, shrug their shoulders and put it down to experience,' says Mr Watson, 49.

'I don't blame them but the trouble is it becomes a vicious circle and so becomes the norm. As a result, it makes it increasingly difficult for graduates to find an actual, paid job.'

For those students graduating this summer [2010] the message is clear—however much work they put into securing a good degree, when it comes to finding a job it probably won't be enough.

In Japan, Internships Can Be Valuable or Exploitative

Terrie Lloyd

Terrie Lloyd is a dual national of Australia and New Zealand and is the chief executive officer of the business magazine Japan, Inc. *In the following viewpoint, Lloyd says that Japanese internships offered by companies to foreign workers provide valuable experience and real value to the companies. However, a government training program providing internships to foreign workers is notoriously exploitative, according to Lloyd. Lloyd argues that the government should come up with a fair and nonexploitative standardized internship program.*

As you read, consider the following questions:

1. According to Lloyd, what do internships conventionally mean for Westerners?
2. According to Lloyd, why is a company he is familiar with hiring dozens of Chinese trainees?
3. Why does Lloyd argue that internships should be three months long rather than three to four weeks?

A major staffing company called FujiStaff Holdings has just set up a new subsidiary, called Inter Agent, which will find internships at Japanese firms for foreign students. Inter

Terrie Lloyd, "Internships—Slave Labor or a Worthwhile Experience?," *Japan Today*, July 31, 2010. Reproduced by permission of Japan Inc. Communications. Reprinted by permission of the author.

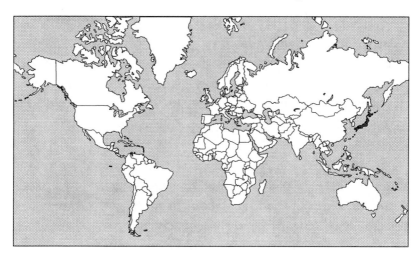

Agent is apparently wanting to take advantage of the fact that there are around 130,000 foreign students studying in Japan at any given time and many of them want to stay on and get jobs after they graduate.

Foreign Workers in Japan

The timing is such that those larger companies which are on a major globalization push are obviously going to be looking for Japanese-speaking foreigners who can learn the company's methods and processes, and eventually get assigned positions in that firm's holdings abroad. As an example, Panasonic has said that next spring it plans for 80% of its new hires to be from applicants who are non-Japanese.

Actually, staffing giant Pasona Group started a similar business back in 1988, helping Westerners studying in Japan to find work experience at Japanese firms. In 2007, they moved to take applications from China and Taiwan, and in 2009, 620 of those applying for internships came from those two countries—although only eight were accepted to finally take up actual internships. The reasons for the low acceptance rate were as always, language and prior work skills.

But while FujiStaff and Pasona are still looking for the right formula to get more foreigners into the workforce via internships and trainee positions, there are already plenty of companies tapping into the foreign student resources pool. According to the Immigration Bureau, 10,277 foreign students in 2008 changed from student status to either an engineering visa or a humanities visa.

I don't know how many of these were achieved by internships and trainee positions, but knowing that Japanese companies are typically cautious about bringing in foreign staff, I imagine that many of these students changing status are doing so after becoming known to their future employers by some low-risk means such as doing an internship. Indeed, in my opinion, internships are an ideal method for foreigners to segue into a job with a Japanese employer, because the initial shock of having a foreigner in the ranks is soon overcome by growing familiarity and support from co-workers who generally respect a newcomer for having the gumption to do something challenging in their lives.

Internships mean different things to different people. Conventionally for Westerners it is a nonpaid opportunity for a student or new-to-Japan young person with little or no work experience to work in a company for 1–3 months, with the objective of either gaining recognition on their resume or to eventually gain employment at the company they are doing the internship for.

In my opinion, internships are an ideal method for foreigners to segue into a job with a Japanese employer.

Japanese Firms Going Global

Since the 2008 Lehman shock [referring to the failure of financial firm Lehman Brothers that precipitated a global recession], most larger firms (foreign firms in particular) are more reluctant to give internships, because they realize that the real expense of having an intern is not the cost of the desk and infrastructure, but instead lies in the care and attention the intern needs from existing personnel in order to get trained. This means that internships with foreign firms are more typically found with smaller firms that are looking for a helping hand in return for providing training and experience. However, as FujiStaff and Pasona believe, there is an increasing number of Japanese companies who are committed to going global and therefore have made foreign interns part of their strategic action list.

Last month [June 2010], Mitsui Chemicals announced that [it] has started an internship program for Indian post-grad students in chemistry-related courses to work at company plants in Tokyo and Osaka. Unlike internships at other companies, the Mitsui opportunities will be just four weeks a year, but come with a daily "salary" of 3,000 yen as well as a flat 300,000 yen payment to cover air travel, accommodation, and food.

Another company that has an internship program is Rakuten, which last year [2009] took on 300 new graduates. In their case, the internships are available for certain job classifications while the students are still at school. Their main requirement is that if a foreign student is applying, that they are able to communicate in Japanese—an interesting requirement, given that the company has now committed to making all internal communication in English by 2012.

I've seen a number of less well-known companies work aggressively to bring in foreign students in Japan with the intention of signing them up as employees. One major firm I am familiar with has dozens of Chinese trainees and some full-time employees, with the stated goal of sending them back to China in the future to represent the company with their Japanese customers in that country. I imagine that this same scenario is happening among the hundreds of Japanese

---

Worked to Death in Japan

The day before he [Nobuo Miura] collapsed he had worked from 11 AM until 4:30 AM the next morning, but had managed to snatch a few hours' sleep before starting again. But when Miura, 47, tried to pick up his hammer and nails again, he suddenly took ill. He died a week later. Last week [June 2008] a coroner returned a verdict of "karoshi": death by overwork.

Esther Addley and Laura Barton,
"Karoshi—Death by Overworking," Brand Tao (blog),
January 20, 2008. http://brandtao.wordpress.com.

---

corporations who are now expanding breakneck into Asia and elsewhere. It's not hard, then, to see who is hiring those 10,000 foreign students a year.

I've seen a number of less well-known companies work aggressively to bring in foreign students in Japan with the intention of signing them up as employees.

Slave Labor

Then there is the "other" definition of internship in Japan: which is one of virtual slave labor. I am referring to the foreign trainee and technical internship program established by the government some years ago to allow 200,000 young people from developing countries to learn on the job at Japanese companies. After three years of such "work experience," these workers are supposed to return home again, armed with their newfound knowledge.

Of course, the reality is sadly different, as was exposed through the death through overwork ("karoshi") of a 31-year-old Chinese trainee in June 2008. The Ibaraki labor standards office found that the trainee died from overwork, after having done over 100 hours of overtime every month in the three months prior to his death. The Japan International Training Cooperation Organization reckons that 35 trainees died during FY[fiscal year]2008, with 16 dying of causes symptomatic of "karoshi." In FY2009, 27 such trainees died.

These government-sponsored traineeships/internships do come with salary, which I suppose makes them marginally better than a standard internship—except for the fact that they run for years versus weeks. But the amounts paid are so low, typically around 100,000 yen/month for the first couple of years, that they can hardly be conducive to learning on the job. Rather they create an atmosphere of desperation that obviates any original purpose for people coming in on the program. Instead, the interns become a source of underpaid labor for small manufacturers who would otherwise go out of business.

Then there is the "other" definition of internship in Japan: which is one of virtual slave labor.

Genuine internships, on the other hand, are supposed to be a fair and reasonable trade of personal effort by the intern over a short period of time in return for training and work experience by the company offering the internship. While some people think that 3–4 weeks should be long enough for an internship, I think that three months is a more reasonable exchange. My reasoning for this is simple: If the purpose of the internship is to gain meaningful experience and to perhaps prove oneself to a future employer, anything that can be taught in less than 2–3 months is probably not going to amount to much of value to either the intern or the employer.

There has to be a limit, of course, and rationally, this would be the amount of time that it takes for a potential employer to decide that the intern is the right material for a hire. 2–3 months is plenty of time to make this decision, and by no coincidence is also the same amount of time given to a company to decide whether or not to retain or fire a new employee. It also happens to be the amount of time most students have off before having to return to school after the summer break.

The question inevitably comes up of whether interns should be paid, especially since regular new employees are paid for their services. My response is that if the person applying for the internship has no obvious skills or experience to warrant their applying for an open position, the chance of companies even interviewing such people is low. Whereas, someone starting on an internship is able to show growth and on-the-job aptitude, and so have a chance to convince those they are working with that it is worthwhile extending a job offer to them.

Before anyone complains how evil unpaid internships are, consider that not only are they completely voluntary, but that many well-known organizations provide such opportunities. You may be surprised, for example, to know that the U.S. government's Foreign Commercial Service in Japan offers unpaid internships. . . .

Now that only 80% of this year's university graduates were able to land jobs before leaving school, maybe it's time for the unemployed 20%, the government, and smaller Japanese companies to come up with a standardized internship/work experience program that will help both sides. In particular, the government needs to recognize the difference between internships and paid employment, so that issues of compensation are dealt with and all parties realize the full value of the internship system. They also need to introduce a more specific type of visa for foreign interns, who otherwise have to come in either on a visitor visa (in which case they definitely can't get paid) or they are forced into one of the above mentioned much-abused trainee visas.

Child Sex Trafficking in Malaysia Is a Serious Problem

ECPAT International

ECPAT International is a global network of organizations and individuals working together for the elimination of child sexual exploitation. In the following viewpoint, ECPAT says that Malaysian children are victims of trafficking and are forced to work as sex slaves. ECPAT says that this inhumane and unjust practice must cease. The organization argues that the Malaysian government should do more to enforce anti-trafficking laws and should ratify international laws protecting children.

As you read, consider the following questions:

1. According to ECPAT, to what countries are Malaysian children trafficked, and from what countries are children trafficked to Malaysia?
2. What does ECPAT say about the profile of those who exploit children?
3. What does ECPAT recommend Malaysia do to prevent child trafficking and protect victims of trafficking?

Human trafficking is a complex phenomenon fueled by the tremendous growth in the global sex market. Exploitation is driven by poverty, uneven development, official cor-

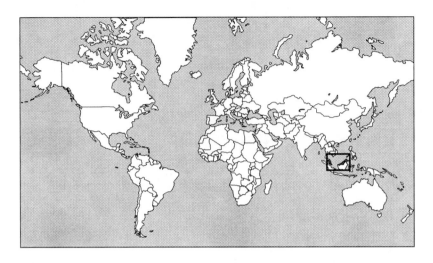

ruption, gender discrimination, harmful traditional and cultural practices, civil unrest, natural disasters and lack of political will to end it.

Trafficking Is a Multibillion-Dollar Industry

The number of child victims trafficked worldwide for sexual exploitation or cheap labour on an annual basis is 1.2 million. Human trafficking, the third largest international crime, following illegal drugs and arms trafficking, is believed to be worth billions of dollars each year. Driving the trade is the demand for commercial sexual exploitation. Seventy-nine percent of all global trafficking is for sexual exploitation.

Although the trafficking of children for sexual purposes has been covered in the news and in other reports in Malaysia, statistical data on the number of trafficked children to and from the country is very scarce. A church study estimated that there are approximately 30–32,000 trafficked persons in the Sabah area alone, although the data did not disaggregate the number of trafficked children from adults. The United Nations Office on Drugs and Crime (UNODC) reported that from 2003 to 2006, about 160 people were convicted of child abduction and child trafficking. The majority of them were involved particularly in trafficking of children for sexual exploitation.

Children are especially vulnerable to being trafficked because they are often uneducated, easy to overpower and easy to convince.

Malaysian children and women are trafficked to Singapore, Hong Kong, Taiwan, Japan, Canada, USA, Europe and Australia for prostitution. Likewise, women and children from Cambodia, China, Colombia, Ecuador, India, Indonesia, Laos, Myanmar, the Philippines, Russia, Thailand, Uzbekistan and Vietnam are trafficked to Malaysia for commercial sexual exploitation and forced labour. Girls from indigenous groups and rural areas in Malaysia are also internally trafficked for the same purposes.

The demand for sex drives child sex trafficking globally while poverty, domestic violence and abuse, discrimination and the desire for a better life makes children vulnerable. Children are especially vulnerable to being trafficked because they are often uneducated, easy to overpower and easy to convince. Children may also be in a position where they feel they must help to support their families and may be sold or sent abroad by family members to do so. Street children, children in refugee camps, children whose family and community life has been disrupted and do not have someone to look out for them are all especially vulnerable to human trafficking.

Children may be at greater risk of trafficking from places where they are less protected. This may be because the law is weak or not properly enforced or because children are less aware of the risks of trafficking and are more easily deceived. Countries are considered:

- 'Sending' or 'origin'—from where children are sent;

- 'Transit'—where the children might be moved through and temporarily kept on the way to their final destination; and

- 'Receiving' or 'destination'—where the children finally end up.

Depending on the reason for trafficking, some countries might be only sending, while others might be both sending and transit. Some countries can be all three. Malaysia is a source, transit and destination country for trafficking of women and children.

Case Study: Three young women aged from 18 to 23 were sent back to Cambodia on 3 July 2007 after being rescued by Malaysian police from a brothel in November 2006. They were forced into prostitution in Malaysia for several years; one of the three was tricked by her sister, while she was in Cambodia, into getting a job in Malaysia in 2006 and then sold into prostitution (information on the other two was not immediately available). Deputy Minister of Women's Affairs of the Royal Government of Cambodia stated that "at least 51 Cambodian girls and women were rescued from brothels in Malaysia from 2005–2007".

Bisexually Exploiting Children

Traffickers prey on children and young people to meet the sexual demands of paedophiles and people who pay for sex. Any person who patronises the commercial sex market may end up sexually exploiting a child. There is no common profile of perpetrators who sexually exploit children—they may be young, old, married, single; they come from all types of socioeconomic backgrounds and work in all kinds of professions.

Traffickers can be a stranger or someone the child knows, such as a relative or a friend. Traffickers are often part of an organised criminal network that 'recruits' children and supplies them with fake identification. They may also pose as boyfriends or girlfriends in order to convince children to leave for a new life. In Malaysia, transnational organised crime groups are believed to be involved in the trafficking of Malaysian children to other countries and arranging illegal entry into Malaysia.

Any person who patronises the commercial sex market may end up sexually exploiting a child.

Case Studies:

- Following a two-month joint operation between Indonesian and Malaysian police, a Malaysian businessman and three Indonesians belonging to a trafficking network were arrested for trafficking teenage girls from Jakarta to Malaysia through Borneo island using false travel documents. Achmad Rifai, head of the Jakarta city police women and children's division, stated that the group confessed to transporting 25 teenagers. The girls, aged 14 to 17, were promised jobs in Jakarta as domestic workers, but were instead forced into sex work. Only six of the 25 girls had been rescued at the time of the report.

- A woman known as Khun Thea was sentenced to 85 years' imprisonment for luring Cambodian girls into prostitution. Two of the trafficked victims revealed that they were 16 years old at the time of the incident. They were looking for pocket money for the New Year and were told by their neighbor that they would get good pay for washing dishes in a Bangkok restaurant. They were trafficked across the border in the back of a pickup truck, covered by a tarpaulin. Once in Bangkok, they were taken to an apartment before being trafficked again to Kuala Lumpur [Malaysia]. One was forced to work on the streets, the other in a karaoke bar. After a few months on the streets, one of the girls was arrested. She spent a year in prisons and detention centres in Malaysia and Thailand and was finally deported back to Cambodia. The other girl asked the Malaysian police for help but was sold across the border to a Thai police unit. There she was forced to work off her debt to the police in another bar, before finally finding her way home. The United Nations has hailed the case as a breakthrough since it was the most substantial sentence ever given in Southeast Asia as punishment for engaging in human trafficking.

The [Malaysian] government must increase efforts to prosecute and convict state officials who receive benefits from or are involved in trafficking and/or exploit potential victims.

Stopping the Trafficking of Children

Law and Law Enforcement:

- While the government of Malaysia has anti-trafficking legislation in place and has developed support services for trafficked victims, it needs to fully implement and enforce the law to tackle multi-dimensional aspects of trafficking by discreetly distinguishing trafficked victims from migrant workers and people arrested for prostitution.

- Ensure trafficking victims are protected from threats and punishment related to acts committed as a result of being trafficked.

Sources of Foreign Victims of Human Trafficking to US States

China,
Hong Kong,
Myanmar,
Taiwan,
Thailand,
Dominican Rep.,
Mexico,
Czech Rep.,
Hungary

Hong Kong,
South Korea,
Taiwan,
Thailand

China,
Malaysia,
Thailand,
Vietnam

China,
Malaysia,
Thailand,
Vietnam,
Belarus, Latvia

China,
Malaysia,
Thailand,
Vietnam

WA

(CT) Korea,
Taiwan,
Hong Kong,
Thailand

NY

NV

IL IN OH PA

(NJ) Mexico

CA

CO

KY VA

AZ

TN NC

(MD) Russia,
Ukraine

China, India,
Malaysia,
Thailand,
Mexico

TX

GA

Mexico

(DC) Thailand,
Vietnam, Malaysia,
Dominican Rep.,
China

FL

China, Malaysia,
Thailand, Vietnam,
Honduras,
Guatemala

China, Malaysia,
Thailand, Vietnam,
Brazil, Costa Rica,
Mexico, Russia

Based on data from Polaris Project

TAKEN FROM: Human Trafficking Awareness Coalition in Sarasota County, "Florida Is One of Top Three Human Trafficking Destinations in U.S.," 2009. http://htsrq.weebly.com.

- The government must increase efforts to prosecute and convict state officials who receive benefits from or are involved in trafficking and/or exploit potential victims.

- Malaysia should ratify the *Optional Protocol on the sale of children, child prostitution and child pornography* and *Optional Protocol on the involvement of children in armed conflict.*

Prevention of Child Trafficking and Victim Protection and Assistance:

- The government of Malaysia needs to develop protection mechanisms for victims of trafficking by providing psychological consultation and rehabilitation/ reintegration support.

- The government must conduct awareness campaigns on human trafficking to increase the public's understanding about the issues, and provide simplified and concise information about penalties for committing the crimes.

- The government must develop concrete measures to tackle demand for commercial sexual exploitation of children, especially on the increase of sex tourism in the region and harms of children on the Internet.

- The government needs to establish a free helpline, 24-hour services for children experiencing violence, abuse and neglect and ensure that all child victims receive adequate care and counselling, recovery and rehabilitation assistance.

Sex Workers Face Bias in Migration Policies

Susie Bright, in an interview with Laura Agustín

Susie Bright is an American writer on sexuality. Laura Agustín is a sociologist, writer, and academic. In the following viewpoint, Bright and Agustín argue that sex trafficking is an imprecise term that fails to adequately describe the needs or experiences of migrants. Instead, they say, most migrants need particular resources, not "rescuing" by human rights organizations. Bright and Agustín argue that focusing on prostitution and victimization is condescending and unhelpful to migrants.

As you read, consider the following questions:

1. What do Bright and Agustín say is the problem with the term "trafficking"?

2. In what ways do people who decide to try their luck abroad need to be flexible and adaptable, according to Bright and Agustín?

3. What parallels do Bright and Agustín say there are between those who sell sex for money and other occupations?

For quite some time, we've heard about the sex slaves—the traffickers, the sexual bondage emerging at the border. The discovery makes free citizens sick; we feel like we must do anything to make it stop, to uncover the beast.

Susie Bright, in an interview with Laura Agustín, "Sex at the Margins with Laura Agustín," *Susie Bright's Journal*, October 9, 2007. Reprinted by permission of the author.

Few Victims Found

But something very weird has been happening. Last month [September 2007] in the *Washington Post*, a shocking story[1] appeared: *Human Trafficking Evokes Outrage, Little Evidence: U.S. Estimates Thousands of Victims, but Efforts to Find Them Fall Short.*

What?

It turns out nearly 30 million dollars was spent, in a passionate effort, to find a relative[ly] tiny number of victims. The "experts" had estimated over 50,000 sex slaves, then up to a million, and warned of a tidal wave on the horizon. Yet over ten years, and aggressive funding, the activists on the ground found closer to a thousand undocumented workers who matched the description of who they were looking for.

Of course, even one person found in bondage is more than enough. But the politics and polemics of rescue seemed strangely out of whack. Other reporters had raised a red flag years before: see Debbie Nathan's "Oversexed,"[2] and Daniel Radosh's critique of "Bad Trade."[3]

When well-intended social workers and enforcement agents sought out female migrant workers with grievances, they often found people who said, "I'm desperate for papers, but I'm not doing sex work—I'm in a different sort of bondage!"

It turns out nearly 30 million dollars was spent, in a passionate effort, to find a relative[ly] tiny number of victims.

Or, they found migrants who said, "I am doing sex work, but I'm making it worth my while, and the one way you could help me is by either getting out of my way or getting me legal documents so I make my own decision." Or, they found male prostitutes who didn't fit the feminine portrait of victimization at all, and they weren't eligible for "help," either. The problem as conceived by the policy makers was completely mismatched with the reality.

Author Laura Agustín[4] has written a new book, *Sex at the Margins: Migration, Labour Markets and the Rescue Industry*,[5] which rethinks the arguments of this entire tableau. If you've EVER read a story about trafficking, "immigration problems," and felt like you didn't know where to turn, this book will turn every assumption you might have on its head. . . .

I interviewed Laura in California this week [October 2007] as her book makes its American debut.

Prejudice Against Prostitutes

Susie Bright: How did you get involved in this subject, of sex work and crossing borders?

Laura Agustín: I'd been working in NGO [nongovernmental organization] projects in the Caribbean, South America and on the Mexico-US border, and I was profoundly dissatisfied.

Too often, funder psychology assumes that poor people are naïve or simple—what a lot of money is wasted on useless projects!

I spent a year in the early '90s wandering around Europe listening to this—pitying, victimizing stories about migrants and people living in poor countries in general.

It was a turning point in my life when I decided to leave the NGO world.

I wanted to know why there was such a big difference between what migrants said about themselves, and what Europeans said about them, and I couldn't begin to understand why there was such prejudice toward women who sell sex.

Traditional prostitution debates are theoretical, focusing on the abstract question of whether selling sex can be considered a job—or must be defined as violence against women.

Often debates seem to be a search for a single moral truth, in which the words of the subjects themselves are irrelevant.

Those committed to stopping commercial sex are certain of their own ideas and don't trust those of anyone who actually works in the sex industry. They accuse people like me of selling out to patriarchy, being paid by pornographers, or being a pimp, and they accuse professional sex workers of having false consciousness or being irrelevant elites. They believe there is an essence that all biological women have in common—and they know what that essence is. They feel comfortable talking about women's experiences across all cultural and linguistic boundaries. Fundamentalisms are on the rise, and this is one of them.

I wanted to know why there was such a big difference between what migrants said about themselves, and what Europeans said about them.

What did you think of the recent Post *story?*

The bedlam they describe comes about because there is no single definition of "trafficking," that everyone can agree on. The overall issue is migration, the difficulty of crossing borders to work legally.

However, there are so many undocumented workers filling available jobs, that they are likely as numerous as migrants with the full portfolio of papers. Many kinds of travel and employment are unregulated, and all sorts of abuses and injustices are rampant—but that is not the same as saying that all informal migrants are mistreated.

The problem with the term "trafficking" (defined as horrible crime and exploitation), comes when it's applied to everyone, or to all women migrants who sell sex.

This is what all the argument is about. Some people wish to grant a degree of choice and preference to poor people and migrants—and some who do not.

The US government judges the rest of the world annually on their efforts to stop trafficking. Local, national and international organizations allot millions to projects that promise to find and rescue victims of trafficking; hundreds of groups have been founded for this purpose. Their language is evangelistic, and the general public assumes that "Good is Being Done."

But these missionaries do not ask people whether they want to be rescued. Many migrants don't welcome their efforts, including poor women of different ethnic and religious beliefs. Rescuers focus the media's attention on the dramatic moment of "rushing in to liberate slaves," rather than the oppressive process of detention, interrogation, and forced rehabilitation that the rescuers themselves impose.

The issue is not whether terrible experiences occur or not—of course, they do. But it's clear to longtime researchers in the field that the tragic cases are a minority and very rarely fatal. My own interest is not in trafficking but rather in how labor markets and sexualities come to play roles in migration.

When I began, thank goodness "trafficking" was not yet a big panic, or I might never have continued my study.

It should be obvious that no one can get reliable data when people's travels and jobs are unregulated or illegal. Numbers of undocumented migrants can only be guessed at, and they are moving around and changing jobs all the time.

In Germany last year, for example, frightened feminists estimated that 40,000 women would be trafficked in, to serve fans of the World Cup. Swedish government research afterward showed that there had never been any basis for such an estimate and that few cases of trafficking had been found.

Migration vs. Immigration

It's hard to ask you questions without thinking about the language I'm using. The word "migration," as opposed to immigration, for example. It used to be in vogue to say "undocumented workers," and of course there are still people saying "illegal aliens."

Some fish and birds are described as migratory because they travel between places with regularity. Using the word migration instead of immigration refers to the realization that many human beings do the same thing—they leave one place for another, which they then leave again, and perhaps return to, again.

Immigration refers to an idea that people make a final decision to leave home and settle somewhere else. Because of the ease of travel now, and because richer countries are making it so hard to officially enter and stay and settle, the word migration is more accurate. But lots of people don't think of themselves as either immigrants or migrants!

There's always a search for terms that aren't derogatory to people on the fringes of mainstream society, in this case those who have gotten inside extra-legally.

"Alien" is a word used centuries ago. Many are offended by the term "illegal;" some scholars prefer to say, "irregular." "Undocumented" sounds more neutral (in France there is a "sans-papiers" movement), but many of those working illegally do have some papers—passports, permits, visas.

Is it appropriate to say that most major migration today is groups of people fleeing an untenable situation?

No, most people are not "fleeing," but rather have decided to try their luck somewhere else, where they've heard there are more opportunities to get ahead. It's estimated that about 3% of the world's total population migrates.

In places where there's a disaster under way, many more people are displaced, but they might not go far away, and they return as soon as they can.

Even in the worst situations, only certain people leave their countries altogether, and they are not the poorest and most desperate. Migration requires planning, money, and social networks to succeed.

People do a lot of desperate things when they don't have their own leverage. We get the impression from the mainstream media that migrants who arrive penniless in another country are willing to do "anything." So what, really, is the "do anything" that poor migrants are faced with?

Most people do not arrive penniless, they arrive with their own or borrowed money, even if the amounts don't seem large to richer people.

They arrive with a plan, they've got the names and telephone numbers or addresses of people they already know, or have been referred to.

Characterization of everyone as "desperate" is not helpful if you want to de-victimize and acknowledge mirgants' skills and desires to get ahead—however they define it.

If you focus solely on the moment of crossing the border—for example, between Mexico and Arizona—then it all looks like violent drama and desperation. However, most crossings are uneventful and people move on, without the media or vigilantes ever seeing them.

That doesn't mean they didn't have to borrow a big amount of money or go through scary moments along the way, and it doesn't mean these are all happy endings.

But the characterization of everyone as "desperate" is not helpful if you want to de-victimize and acknowledge migrants' skills and desires to get ahead—however they define it.

People who decide to try their luck abroad, need to be flexible and adaptable in how they will live. They'll have to share space with people in a way they wouldn't at home, eat strange food, navigate without understanding much of the language around them, deal with loneliness, and take available jobs.

A lot of the jobs offered them are low status: busboy, farm worker, maid. Some people are temporarily grateful to get these jobs, but plan to get out and move up as soon as they can. Making money to pay back debts and send home becomes the priority.

Sex Is Singled Out

Why is it that high-risk sex work options are the "desperate measures" that get all the attention? If I go to work in a sweat shop, or get exploited as a indentured servant, it's all ho-hum— but if I get exploited within something called "the sex industry," then it's worthy of outcry. How do we get people to stop looking for the sexual moral in every migration dilemma?

Sex always gets more attention, don't you think?

I wouldn't agree with your use of "high risk." There are risks in selling sex and there are risks in being a live-in maid, picking ground crops, selling pirated or stolen goods or drugs, working in sweatshops. It's not a good idea to generalize. They are all unregulated jobs with no insurance, no security, no workplace health and safety, and personal dependence on the boss.

People are concerned about the risk in selling sex when they believe that sex is different from every other human experience, or that it is sacred, that it belongs in the same room with love and should never be tainted by money. Some people think that women are sexually vulnerable by definition, always in danger of being violated.

But not everyone feels that way. Some migrants who sell sex do hate what they are doing, but stay on because the money is better and faster than in any other job they can get. Some don't mind selling sex because they learn how to "act" it, and keep it separate from the rest of their lives. Some like doing it. Everyone does not feel the same way about sex.

Men and women selling sex account for a large percentage of migrants, certainly. Notice I'm not talking just about women.

The societal fears about "damage" only get applied to women, so the attention goes to them, but men, transsexuals, and transgenders work in large numbers selling sex, possibly making up half of the total.

Of course, being sexually taken advantage of in a servant ca-pacity or a bottom-of-the-barrel factory situation is par for the course, but again, because it is not prostitution per se.

True. People in low-status labor are always being pressured to have sex, to keep their jobs—think of the old clichés about secretaries. People in higher-status jobs don't escape pressure either. But migrants in both groups figure out how to use the situation to their own advantage—to make money or contacts out of it.

People are concerned about the risk in selling sex when they believe that sex is different from every other human experience, or that it is sacred.

How does this differ with young men making the same voy-age? How does the masculine experience differ?

The difference is that the policy makers and rescue indus-try are not so concerned about men who sell sex, even to the point of not recognizing they are doing it.

Since men are not thought of as sexually vulnerable, they can get away with more without being pursued by rescuers and police.

Men also sometimes don't get help when they would like some. But it's too misleading to talk about all men versus all women. There are too many different jobs involved, done in a variety of situations with all sorts of personalities and talents. My advice is, don't generalize!

Are you saying, that while no one would elect to work for meager wages in a sexually exploitive situation, it could be a better choice than what they [are] escaping from?

I don't think you'll find a place in my book where I use the "choice" argument or characterize everyone as "escaping" from horrors.

I don't group millions of people into one imaginary category, whether you call it prostitutes, sex workers, or victims of trafficking.

You'll find plenty of places where I quote migrants who do prefer sex jobs to others, and want to be left alone to get on with it. Whether you get high or low wages in your first sex-industry job is a matter of luck, but after a while, if you have skills and talent, you can move, get more autonomy, get a better boss or get out if you want to.

Plenty of middle-class workers feel the same way, both migrants and not migrants. One of the problems in migrating is that your job qualifications from home aren't recognized in your new country—diplomas, certificates, degrees. So you find civil engineers driving taxis, schoolteachers selling sex, nurses being maids.

The Problem with Empowerment

Why does the "empowerment" crowd rub you the wrong way?

The idea of empowerment is that someone gives power to another, or encourages them to take power or find it within themselves.

It's the "politically correct" way of thinking about those at the bottom of the social heap. However, it places emphasis on the helper and her vision of how to help, encourage and show the way—on good intentions.

In the compromised worlds of "Aid" and "Development," first-world entities use their funds to help those less privileged. They spend money to set up offices and pay salaries, many to people who work in offices writing proposals that will allow them to stay in business. These organizations have hierarchies, and those engaged at the grassroots level often are the last to influence how funds will be used.

Those closer to the top know how to write proposals to compete in the funding world. When empowerment comes from above in this way, it's not surprising that money is spent to little effect, such as rescue projects which can't find anyone who wants to be rescued.

By its very nature, your book is going to attract the sort of person who DOES want to make the world better, help people, be a RESCUER! What does a caring person do?

I certainly hope people working in social-justice projects will read the book. Many of them already have doubts and feel caught up in a bureaucratic web, dependent on pleasing funders, or itching to take more relevant action.

Those who want to support undocumented workers have few options for getting funds—AIDS prevention and "rescuing victims of trafficking" are two.

But the undocumented want papers. They want the right to work and rent housing legally, to stop fearing the police or bosses, to be able to get on with their lives, and make money to pay back debts.

It is very frustrating for grassroots educators to know they can't help with any of that.

Those who want to support undocumented workers have few options for getting funds—AIDS prevention and "recusing victims of trafficking" are two.

What should they do? It's a huge structural question, but if social-type workers don't believe they have any power to change things they are in the wrong business.

At the end of my book I suggest that people "leave home"—meaning their mental home, the safe place where [their] cherished ideas about right and wrong go unchallenged. Leave behind nationalisms and religious moralisms—and, above all, the assumption that certain people Know Best how everyone else should behave all over the world.

How much "climbing up the ladder" do you think happens? How many migrants in sex work get out of the game, get out of debt? We always hear about the frightened teenager, held hostage in a brothel ... but I wonder, where are the twenty-year-olds? The thirty- and forty-year-olds?

In my own research I've talked with managers of flats (brothels) who started out working in them, with dancers who used to be on the street and so on. There are also many who would like to get out of prostitution but feel trapped in it—transsexuals are the major group complaining of this.

Sex and Money

So how far do you take the prostitution as work metaphor? Paging Friedrich Engels![7]

[Karl] Marx argued that all workers were prostituted, Engels said that all married women were the same, and many feminists have since made the same argument. It's very difficult to condemn prostitution and then defend dating and marriage, because all mix up money and sex.

There is hardly anything surprising or innovative about combining sex and money, and I do not see any liberatory potential in it per se.

The problem is in the dominant idea of what role sex is "supposed" to play, and the great fear that money contaminates it. This is ridiculous, given the normalized role of money in dating and marriage.

There is hardly anything surprising or innovative about combining sex and money, and I do not see any liberatory potential in it per se.

The fear that those who sell sex are all "exploited" also ignores parallels with other kinds of workers, from maids to football players. Children competing as gymnasts or training to be ballerinas submit to tremendous discipline from others who could equally be thought of as exploiting them. For me, these comparisons are useful in reducing the obsession and stigma attached to prostitution or sex work.

However, many consider sex so absolutely "different" that it cannot be compared to anything else. Some believe that sexuality constitutes personal identity—a Western idea called the "self", which can be damaged by improper use. This is really what makes the traditional prostitution debate futile: a quasi-religious belief that can never be proved and which seems absurd to those who don't share it. There's no point in arguing when such beliefs are at stake.

Links

1. Jerry Markon, "Human Trafficking Evokes Outrage, Little Evidence: U.S. Estimates Thousands of Victims, but Efforts to Find Them Fall Short," *Washington Post*, September 23, 2007. http://www.washingtonpost.com/wp-dyn/content/article/2007/09/22/AR2007092201401_pf.html.

2. Debbie Nathan, "Oversexed," *The Nation*, August 11/August 29, 2005. http://www.thenation.com/article/oversexed.

3. Daniel Radosh, "Bad trade," September 27, 2007. http://s91215004.onlinehome.us/mt/mt-search.cgi?IncludeBlogs=1&search=landesman.

4. Laura Agustín, The Naked Anthropologist, "US Trafficking Office Wants Your Help with Imperialist Anti-Trafficking Operations." http://www.lauraagustin.com.

5. Laura María Agustín, *Sex at the Margins: Migration, Labour Markets and the Rescue Industry.* http://www.amazon.com/dp/ASIN/1842778609/?tag=susiebrightcom.

7. "Friedrich Engels." http://en.wikipedia.org/wiki/Friedrich_Engels#The_Origin_of_the_Family.2C_Private_Property.2C_and_the_State_.281884.29.

Periodical and Internet Sources Bibliography

The following articles have been selected to supplement the diverse views presented in this chapter.

Associated Press   "European Slave Labor Market Could Boom During Slowdown," FoxNews.com, December 2, 2008. www.foxnews.com.

Economist   "The Sex Industry in Cambodia: The Traffic Police," June 11, 2009.

Steven Greenhouse   "The Unpaid Intern, Legal or Not," *New York Times*, April 2, 2010.

Paul Harris   "Forced Labour and Rape, the New Face of Slavery in America," *Observer*, November 22, 2009.

Human Rights Watch   "Middle East: Sri Lankan Domestic Workers Face Abuse," November 14, 2007. www.hrw.org.

Migrant Rights   "Migrant Domestic Workers in the Middle East: Exploited, Abused and Ignored," April 30, 2010. www.migrant-rights.org.

Claire Newell   "Revealed: Topshop Clothes Made with 'Slave Labour,'" *Times*, August 12, 2007.

Brendan O'Neill   "The Myth of Trafficking," *New Statesman*, March 27, 2008.

Julian Ryall   "Japan's 'Slave Labour' Interns Die After 16 Hour Days," *Telegraph*, July 6, 2010.

Sydney Morning Herald   "Slave Labour in the Blue Mountains," July 21, 2006.

Morgan Tanabe   "Are Internships Slave Labor?," Statepress.com, February 5, 2010. www.statepress.com.

For Further Discussion

Chapter 1

1. Based on the viewpoints in this chapter, what are some of the advantages and some of the disadvantages of strong workplace regulations? Would you rather work in an industry that was lightly regulated or heavily regulated? Explain your reasoning.

2. Does the French practice of offering six weeks of vacation time a year seem too generous, not generous enough, or just right? Explain your answer.

Chapter 2

1. Consider the viewpoints by Han Dongfang, Keith Ewing, and Robert Barro. Does it make sense to think of collective bargaining as a human right? Why or why not?

2. Based on the viewpoints in this chapter, how do unions help workers? How do they hurt workers? Do you think that on balance unions do more harm than good, or more good than harm? Explain your answer.

Chapter 3

1. Based on the viewpoints in this chapter, is workplace discrimination a problem for economic reasons or for moral ones? That is, would workplace discrimination hurt companies economically? Explain your answer.

2. Could any workplace discrimination ever be justified? If so, on what grounds? Explain your answer.

Chapter 4

1. Based on the viewpoints in this chapter, is it reasonable to refer to internships as "slave labor"? Explain your reasoning.

2. Laura Agustín argues that policy should focus on helping people cross borders safely and legally rather than focusing on rescuing victims of sex trafficking. Do her arguments seem like they would be applicable to the domestic workers discussed in the viewpoint by Human Rights Watch? Or does the Human Rights Watch viewpoint tend to undermine Agustín's arguments? Explain your answer.

Organizations to Contact

The editors have compiled the following list of organizations concerned with the issues debated in this book. The descriptions are derived from materials provided by the organizations. All have publications or information available for interested readers. The list was compiled on the date of publication of the present volume; the information provided here may change. Be aware that many organizations take several weeks or longer to respond to inquiries, so allow as much time as possible.

All-China Federation of Trade Unions (ACFTU)

10 Fuxingmenwai Street, Beijing   100865
   China
+86-10-68591553/1554 • fax: +86-10-68562031/2039
website: http://english.acftu.org

The All-China Federation of Trade Unions (ACFTU) is the sole national trade union federation of the People's Republic of China. It is the largest trade union federation in the world. The ACFTU seeks to protect the interests of the Chinese people and of workers in particular. It also works to realize the socialist modernization of China. Its website includes news reports, essays, reports, and the magazine *Chinese Trade Unions*.

American Federation of Labor and Congress of Industrial Organizations (AFL-CIO)

815 Sixteenth Street NW, Washington, DC   20006
(202) 637-5000
website: www.aflcio.org

The American Federation of Labor and Congress of Industrial Organizations (AFL-CIO) is the largest federation of unions in the United States. Its mission is to improve the lives of working families by organizing and lobbying for economic and social justice. Its website includes statements, press releases, news updates, essays, and articles about the union movement.

Amnesty International

International Secretariat, London   WC1X 0DW
  United Kingdom
+44-20-74135500 • fax: +44-20-79561157
website: www.amnesty.org

Amnesty International is a grassroots, activist organization that undertakes research and action to prevent and end grave abuses of human rights such as the rights to physical and mental integrity, freedom of conscience and expression, and freedom from discrimination. Its website includes reports and recommendations on human rights issues, including labor and workers' rights.

European Commission—Economic and Financial Affairs (ECOFIN)

Unit A5, Brussels   B-1049
  Belgium
fax: (+32) 2 29 808 23
website: http://ec.europa.eu/economy_finance

The European Commission—Economic and Financial Affairs (ECOFIN) is entrusted with the regulation of European Union (EU) economic and monetary policy. Its goal is to ensure the smooth functioning of economic integration in the EU. Its website includes access to economics forecasts, research papers, news articles on the European economic situation, and links to its electronic publications *European Economy News* and *European Economy Research Letter*.

Heritage Foundation

214 Massachusetts Avenue NE, Washington, DC   20002-4999
(202) 546-4400 • fax: (202) 546-8328
e-mail: info@heritage.org
website: www.heritage.org

The Heritage Foundation is a research and educational institute that promotes conservative public policies based on the principles of free enterprise, limited government, individual freedom, traditional American values, and a strong national defense. Its website includes policy briefs on US agriculture, the economy, health care, the federal budget and spending, labor, retirement and social security, as well as international trade policy and economic freedom.

Human Rights Watch (HRW)
350 Fifth Avenue, 34th Floor, New York, NY   10118-3299
(212) 290-4700 • fax: (212) 736-1300
e-mail: hrwnyc@hrw.org
website: www.hrw.org

Human Rights Watch (HRW) is an international organization dedicated to ensuring that the human rights of individuals worldwide are observed and protected. To achieve this protection, HRW investigates allegations of human rights abuses and then works to hold violators, be they governments or individuals, accountable for their actions. The organization's website is divided by continent, offering specific information on individual countries and issues.

International Labour Organization (ILO)
4 route des Morillons, Genève 22   CH-1211
    Switzerland
+41 (0) 22 799 6111 • fax: +41 (0) 22 798 8685
e-mail: ilo@ilo.org
website: www.ilo.org

The International Labour Organization (ILO) is a United Nations agency that is devoted to advancing opportunities for women and men to obtain decent and productive work in conditions of freedom, equity, security, and human dignity. Its main aims are to promote rights at work, encourage decent employment opportunities, enhance social protection, and strengthen dialogue in handling work-related issues. The ILO publishes numerous publications about global labor, including

Global Employment Trends 2011 and *Towards Decent Work in Sub-Saharan Africa*. Many of these publications are available at ILO's website.

United States Department of Labor

200 Constitution Avenue NW, Washington, DC   20210
866-487-2365
website: www.dol.gov

The United States Department of Labor is the cabinet department responsible for occupational safety, wage and hour standards, unemployment insurance benefits, reemployment services, and some economic statistics. Its website includes numerous articles and reports on workers' rights.

World Bank

1818 H Street NW, Washington, DC   20433
(202) 473-1000 • fax: (202) 477-6391
website: www.worldbank.org

The World Bank seeks to reduce poverty and improve the standards of living of poor people around the world. It promotes sustainable growth and investments in developing countries through loans, technical assistance, and policy guidance. The World Bank produces publications on global labor issues, including *Accountability Through Public Opinion*, the annual *World Development Report*, and the annual *World Development Indicators*.

World Trade Organization (WTO)

Centre William Rappard, Rue de Lausanne 154
Geneva 21   CH-1211
    Switzerland
+41 (0)22 739 51 11 • fax: +41 (0)22 731 42 06
e-mail: enquiries@wto.org
website: www.wto.org

The World Trade Organization (WTO) is a global international organization that establishes rules dealing with the trade between nations. Its mission is to provide a forum for negotiating agreements aimed at reducing obstacles to international trade and ensuring a level playing field for all, thus contributing to economic growth and development. WTO publishes trade statistics, research, studies, reports, the annual *World Trade Report*, and the journal *World Trade Review*. Recent publications, including those focusing on labor and workers' rights, are available on the WTO's website.

Bibliography of Books

Laura María Agustín — *Sex at the Margins: Migration, Labour Markets and the Rescue Industry.* London: Zed Books, 2007.

Sakhela Buhlungu — *A Paradox of Victory: COSATU and the Democratic Transformation in South Africa.* Scottsville, South Africa: University of KwaZulu-Natal Press, 2010.

Isla Carmichael — *Pension Power: Unions, Pension Funds, and Social Investment in Canada.* Toronto, Canada: University of Toronto Press, 2005.

Nicole Constable — *Maid to Order in Hong Kong: Stories of Migrant Workers.* 2nd ed. Ithaca, NY: Cornell University Press, 2007.

Philip Dray — *There Is Power in a Union: The Epic Story of Labor in America.* New York: Doubleday, 2010.

Barbara Ehrenreich and Arlie Russell Hochschild, eds. — *Global Woman: Nannies, Maids, and Sex Workers in the New Economy.* New York: Metropolitan Books, 2003.

Sue Fernie and David Metcalf, eds. — *Trade Unions: Resurgence or Demise?* New York: Routledge, 2005.

Jonathan Franklin — *33 Men: Inside the Miraculous Survival and Dramatic Rescue of the Chilean Miners.* New York: G.P. Putnam's Sons, 2011.

Thomas Geoghegan — *Were You Born on the Wrong Continent? How the European Model Can Help You Get a Life.* New York: New Press, 2010.

James A. Gross, ed. — *Workers' Rights as Human Rights.* Ithaca, NY: Cornell University Press, 2003.

Bernard Harris, Lina Gálvez, and Helena Machado, eds. — *Gender and Well-Being in Europe: Historical and Contemporary Perspectives.* Burlington, VT: Ashgate Publishing Company, 2009.

Siddharth Kara — *Sex Trafficking: Inside the Business of Modern Slavery.* New York: Columbia University Press, 2009.

Katarina Katz — *Gender, Work and Wages in the Soviet Union: A Legacy of Discrimination.* New York: Palgrave, 2001.

Prabha Kotiswaran — *Dangerous Sex, Invisible Labor: Sex Work and the Law in India.* Princeton, NJ: Princeton University Press, 2011.

Gracia Liu-Farrer — *Labour Migration from China to Japan: International Students, Transnational Migrants.* New York: Routledge, 2011.

Matthew Lynn — *Bust: Greece, the Euro and the Sovereign Debt Crisis.* Hoboken, NJ: Bloomington Press, 2011.

Pardis Mahdavi — *Gridlock: Labor, Migration, and Human Trafficking in Dubai.* Stanford, CA: Stanford University Press, 2011.

Reena Patel — *Working the Night Shift: Women in India's Call Center Industry.* Stanford, CA: Stanford University Press, 2010.

Ross Perlin — *Intern Nation: How to Earn Nothing and Learn Little in the Brave New Economy.* New York: Verso Books, 2011.

Tim Pringle — *Trade Unions in China: The Challenge of Labour Unrest.* New York: Routledge, 2011.

Thomas D. Rogers — *The Deepest Wounds: A Labor and Environmental History of Sugar in Northeast Brazil.* Chapel Hill: University of North Carolina Press, 2010.

Dorothy J. Solinger — *States' Gains, Labor's Losses: China, France, and Mexico Choose Global Liaisons, 1980–2000.* Ithaca, NY: Cornell University Press, 2009.

Anne Stangl et al. — *Tackling HIV-Related Stigma and Discrimination in South Asia.* Washington, DC: World Bank, 2010.

Sukhadeo Thorat and Katherine S. Newman, eds. — *Blocked by Caste: Economic Discrimination in Modern India.* New Delhi, India: Oxford University Press, 2010.

Benjamin W. Wolkinson — *Arab Employment in Israel: The Quest for Equal Employment Opportunity.* Westport, CT: Greenwood Press, 1999.

Index

Geographic headings and page numbers in **boldface** refer to viewpoints about that country or region.